Henry Lloyd

The History of the Late War in Germany

Between the King of Prussia, and the Empress of Germany and her allies

Henry Lloyd

The History of the Late War in Germany
Between the King of Prussia, and the Empress of Germany and her allies

ISBN/EAN: 9783337298043

Printed in Europe, USA, Canada, Australia, Japan

Cover: Foto ©ninafisch / pixelio.de

More available books at **www.hansebooks.com**

THE HISTORY

OF THE LATE

WAR IN GERMANY,

BETWEEN THE

KING OF PRUSSIA,

AND THE

EMPRESS OF GERMANY AND HER ALLIES.

HISTORY

OF THE

WAR in GERMANY.

PRELIMINARY DISCOURSE.

IN order to convey a more clear idea of the hiftory of this war, and of its various operations; we think it may be ufeful previoufly to fhew the motives which induced the feveral powers of Europe to undertake it. And alfo to give an exact defcription of the country where it was carried on; becaufe, the knowledge of thefe two points will, it is imagined, enable the the reader to form a proper judgment of the generals who conducted the different armies, and of the propriety of their manœuvres, to obtain the end each had in view.

As the reafons which determined England to declare war againft France are generally known: a detail of them would be needlefs. We fhall therefore relate thofe of other nations only.

Of FRANCE.

THE French convinced from experience, nothing could more effectually contribute to realize that fuperiority, which they arrogated to themfelves in Europe, than the cultivation and improvement of their American colonies, resolved, on concluding the peace of Aix la Chapelle, to promote with care and vigilance every scheme that seemed calculated to distress our, and advance their own settlements. The first step towards accomplishing this end, was to find a means to cut off our communication with the Indians, on whose friendship the greatness of our colonies much depends. This, in the end, would naturally unite them to the French, who could furnish them with what they wanted in exchange for the different commodities of that country, and by degrees be made an instrument to drive us out of it. They begun to execute their plan by establishing a chain of forts behind our settlements, and by occupying many countries, until then, thought, at least neutral. Though they had not as yet compleated it, what was already done had such an influence on our inland trade, as made us tremble at the fatal consequences which would necessarily follow, if we did not, in time, exert ourselves and repel the injuries they intended us. Some measures, though ineffectual, were taken for that purpose, and hostilities were ordered to be committed against the French both in Europe and America. As they were not prepared sufficiently to avow their pretensions, they only opposed remonstrances and a seeming moderation to our repeated attacks. By this means they proposed to gain time, make us relax in our preparations, and render us odious to the other courts of Europe. In all which they succeeded, more or less, as the history of those times, fully evinces.

Finding at length that the contest must be decided by arms, and that however formidable their land army was, the dispute in America was unequal, and would probably be determined in our favour, as it depended intirely on the means of transporting and sustaining an army there, and consequently was intimately connected with a superiority at sea; they wisely formed a scheme for attacking

tacking Hanover; the conquest of which they suppofed eafy, and from the king's natural affection for that country, they hoped a reftitution of it would make them regain whatever they loft in America, or procure them some other advantages. In the mean time their army would be maintained from the contributions to be raifed in the conquered country, and by its pofition on the Elbe, overawe Germany, and effectually give laws to the contending parties.

This plan was in the beginning attended with all the fuccefs imaginable, and in the end was rendered ineffectual, only by the rapacioufnefs and ignorance of the French general who then commanded.

The French fyftem was, we think, well concerted and even great. They had then, including the militia, near 220,000 men, maintained at a great expence; thefe would remain intirely ufelefs, if the war was limited to America, or even to England, for want of a marine, which could not be formed in time of war; and the lefs fo, as we had already acquired too great a fuperiority.

A German War, was for all thefe reafons both eligible and neceffary, the expence of it to them, was comparatively nothing at all, being reduced to the fimple difference, between maintaining an army in the field, and keeping it at home. They had troops fufficient to form an army in Germany, to guard their country, and to conquer America; fuppofing their marine had been capable to protect their tranfports into that country. To fupply this extraordinary expence, they propofed making every country between the Rhine and the Elbe contribute. This they believed would produce more than fufficient for that purpofe; fo that they would have an immenfe army maintained and enriched at the expence of others. Add to this, that being limitrophes, this alone gave them infinite advantages over us.

Whereas if England propofed fending an army into Germany, fhe muft form it out of nothing, that is, fhe had not one man as yet inlifted for that purpofe, and whatever Englifh would be fent there muft be replaced by new levies, in order to carry on the neceffary war in America. As to the Germans, they knew we muft pay for them at an extraordinary price, all which expence muft be paid by England alone, as it was not pofiible fhe could make any conqueft to bear any confiderable part of it. Thefe circumftances, the French naturally fuppofed, would exhauft the nation's treafure, call the king's attention, confequently that of his minifters to the affairs of Germany, relax our preparations for America, produce murmurs in the people, difunion in our counfels, and at laft reduce us to the neceffity of fubmitting to whatever terms they fhould think fit to impofe. To them much more juftly may be applied that remarkable faying, America was conquered in Germany. The only or at leaft the moft probable means they had of faving or conquering America, was to carry on the war with fuccefs in Germany.

It was indifferent to the French, whether they entered Germany as allies to Pruffia, or Auftria, as either would anfwer the object they had in view. It is probable, however, they would have chofe the firft connexion, as they could with more eafe hurt the Auftrians than the Pruffians. Being informed of our alliance with Ruffia, they inftantly fent a minifter to Pruffia to conclude a treaty on the fame footing as that in the war of 1741; but finding we had been forced to renounce the alliance of the former, and embrace that of the latter, they naturally accepted the friendfhip of the two imperial courts, and under pretence of fulfilling their engagements contracted by this new alliance, they immediately prepared an army of above 100,000 men, about 20,000 of which were deftined to

march

march to the Mayn, and from thence where the emprefs fhould choofe; the remainder, which was to form the main army, was ordered to the lower Rhine, and from thence proceed againſt Hannover and its allies. The command of this army was given to Marſhal D'Etries, as a recompenſe for having negotiated the treaty of Verſailles; and had not the favour of an intriguing miſtreſs prevailed in the choice of thoſe employed afterwards to execute the French plan, all the efforts of England and its allies though ſupported by ſome of the ableſt generals, that this or any age has produced, could not in all probability have prevented its future ſucceſs.

Of AUSTRIA.

THE empreſs had ever reflected on the loſs of Sileſia with infinite regret, being attended with a very great diminution of her revenues and power. Theſe thoughts were aggravated by obſerving the aſcendancy which this additional power gave the king of Pruſſia, whom it is ſaid ſhe perſonally diſliked: ſhe ſaw him treated every where with reſpect, feared and courted by moſt of the courts in Europe. No wonder therefore, that animated with theſe ſentiments, ſhe ſhould form a plan for recovering Sileſia. This ſeems to have been the chief object of her counſels, ever ſince ſhe had ceded it to Pruſſia, as appears evident, from the papers publiſhed by the king on this ſubject. She applied to the empreſs of Ruſſia, and irritated that princeſs againſt the king of Pruſſia to ſuch a degree, that ſhe was eaſily prevailed upon to concur in any meaſures concerted for his ruin. The two imperial Courts were therefore united, by new and ſtrong alliances: the object of which was very extenſive, and tended not only to the recovery of

Sileſia;

Silesia; but to annihilate the king of Prussia, whose dominions they proposed dividing among them. The better to accomplish this end, they invited the king of Poland to accede to this alliance. He however declined it, till he saw the two empresses act with such vigour, as would make it safe for him to declare against Prussia. Experience had taught him that the Prussians could oppress him with more ease and facility, than the Austrians protect him.

The Austrian minister at Petersburg had contributed all he could to the success of the treaty of subsidy between that court and England, with a view to make us, as usual, pay the expence of those Troops, which the two imperial courts intended to employ only for their own particular service in attacking Prussia, and thereby facilitate the recovery of Silesia. Probably things would have gone to their wishes, if the king of Prussia had not declared he would consider as enemies those who brought any foreign troops into the empire; which indicated plainly he would not only hinder the Russians from coming to the succour of Hannover in case of need, but would perhaps treat that electorate as an enemy's country. The king of England very justly considered, that the Russians would be of no use to him, to protect his German dominions, if they were at war with Prussia. For whatever success they might have on the Baltick against that prince, they could never hinder him, being so very near, from occupying the electorate, a country without any natural or artificial strength.

For which reason his majesty very prudently, as we think, preferred the friendship of Prussia, and renounced to that of the two empresses. That of Germany, for whose advantage alone the alliance with Russia had been made, being thus disappointed, easily persuaded the other to break her treaty with us; and the more so, as these courts never had any other object in forming it, than

to receive

to receive a subsidy that would enable them to carry their schemes against Prussia into execution, and by no means to act in concert with us, but on condition we concurred likewise in the plan they had formed for his ruin. Our connexions therefore with him, brought the treaty with Russia to nothing, and very naturally produced another alliance between the two imperial courts and that of France, whose views we have already explained.

Of PRUSSIA.

THE late king of Prussia had cultivated the arts of peace, I mean those which fall more particularly under the cognizance of a prince, justice and interior policy, from principle. The military art rather for shew, than with any particular view, or love of glory. He had left at his death 67,000 men well disciplined, and his magazines abundantly furnished with artillery, stores, &c.

The death of the then emperor Charles VI. left the affairs of the house of Austria, in the utmost confusion, and distress. This the king of Prussia thought a favourable opportunity to assert the claims he had to some part of Silesia, and by such a bold enterprize, at the beginning of his reign, satisfy the ambition he had, to appear a formidable and enterprising power, capable to hold the ballance of the empire, and protect those princes who should hereafter recur to him for succour. He was the first who began the war against the empress, which having succeeded to his wish, he concluded by a treaty that gave him all Silesia.

The recovery of this most fruitful province had been the principal object of the Austrian counsels ever since, which finished, as we have already related in an alliance with Russia calculated for that end. Though they had for many years been occupied by this one

object

object, yet in 1756, they were not prepared to put it in execution, and had fixed the following year for that purpose.

The king of Pruffia perfectly informed of what they had projected againſt him, thought it prudent to anticipitate their operations, and attack the principal power of the confederacy, whom, being as yet unprepared, he hoped to cruſh, and thereby diſſolve the league before they could unite and bring their plan to bear. With this view he entered Saxony: This brought on the general war in Germany, of which we propoſe giving an exact account in the following Work.

Of SAXONY.

AVARICE, an impotent ambition, a ſpirit of intrigue combined with indolence, a total neglect of every thing that tended to the welfare and intereſt of the country, an immoderate love for ſhews, pleaſures, and pageantry, had been long the characteriſtics of this court. No wonder! the man who governed in the name of a too indulgent maſter, had brought with him into the miniſtry thoſe habits he had contracted while a page. Attendance coſt him nothing, his life had been diſſipated in the idle and trifling occupations of a courtier; his great and indeed only talent was the profuſion of an eaſtern monarch, which his vile partiſans called magnificence. He was aſſiduous only in beſieging his royal maſter, to prevent truth and virtue from approaching him; ſo that this humane and good prince, who had the greateſt deſire to promote the good of his people, was never permitted to know they were unhappy and wanted his protection. Though this miniſter knew

that

in GERMANY.

that the abject state, to which his bad conduct had reduced Saxony, made it impossible for him to undertake any thing of consequence. He was, however, always intriguing with the courts of Vienna, and Petersburg, and forming projects for aggrandising Saxony, at the expence of Prussia without having prepared any one means of realising this vain chimera, or even provided for the common defence of the country. The money raised with difficulty on the poor subject, to provide an army for his defence, was dissipated in building magnificent palaces for the favourite, in expensive journeys, &c. to satisfy his abject and low vanity: so that the country, which might easily raise and maintain an army of 50,000 men, had scarce 15,000 without artillery or magazines; and therefore fell an easy prey to an ambitious and powerful invader.

Of RUSSIA.

THOUGH the plan, formed and pursued with unwearied activity and vigilance by Peter the Great, had not since his death, been cultivated with equal care and success; however, what he had already done, made this empire powerful; and therefore respected and caressed. The vast extent of this empire, the variety of its productions, and the number of its inhabitants, form so many and such great sources of power, that a small neglect, which in lesser states would be immediately and severely felt, pass in this country unnoticed, and produce no sensible or direct bad effect. Its resources are so many, that in some measure they may be said to supply those mistakes which happen in the administration, and have kept up the luftre of the empire, though the plan of the firft Peter has not been fteadily adhered to.

While the Ottoman empire was formidable, this court and that of Vienna were naturally connected. The fear of a common, and powerful enemy, united them by the ftrong tye of mutual fafety. Since the decline of the Turkifh empire, fhe finds it no lefs neceffary to cultivate the friendfhip of other princes, particularly that of the maritime powers, who take off a vaft quantity of ufelefs commodities. This brings a proportionable fum of money into the empire, which, there circulating, puts that vaft machine in motion, and renders it therefore formidable. Hence the facility, or rather avidity with which the northern powers in general embrace every opportunity of taking fubfidies. The luxury and magnificence of their courts are thereby kept up, and their princes abundantly fupplied with all the fuperfluities, which vanity has made neceffary, and their armies maintained at the expence of others. To thefe general motives may be added others, the late emprefs of Ruffia had, as we have already faid, conceived a moft violent averfion to the king of Pruffia, and therefore readily concurred in any meafure concerted for his humiliation, and the more fo, as they flattered her with the hopes of extending her dominions on the Baltick, a thing long aimed at, by the Ruffians; fhe therefore with pleafure contracted an alliance with us, which would enable her to execute the defigns of her hatred and politicks at our expence. But finding we would not break with Pruffia, fhe inftantly renounced our friendfhip, and embraced that of France, who promifed her fuch fubfidies, as would enable her to put her troops in motion, and act according to her own principle.

No country

Of SWEDEN.

NO country has in so short a time changed the principles of its constitution so much as this, except Denmark. Sweden in a very few years, from a most despotick government, as it was in Charles the XIIth's time, is now the most limited monarchy in Europe. Denmark, on the contrary, in near the same period, from a free government, is become intirely despotick. Neither seems to have got much by the revolution, as the power and credit of either does not appear to have been thereby augmented at home or abroad, particularly Sweden, whose interests in foreign courts is much sunk. The power of the crown is too limited, and that of the different states which form the constitution, too complicated, to admit of any plan that requires wisdom in deliberation, and vigour in the execution. An attempt was made some years ago to change the constitution, by augmenting the power of the crown, which could not have been executed without endangering the lives and fortunes of many: it was discovered in time, and some of the authors punished; as those who endeavour to subvert the constitution in favour of tyranny justly deserve. Though the plot was rendered vain, it left, however, an universal spirit of discontent, not to say hatred and animosity against the court, whom they naturally supposed had favoured at least, if not promoted a plot, calculated merely to augment the influence of the crown. They seemed particularly exasperated against the queen, a woman of superior talents, and sister to the king of Prussia, to whose instigation they attributed the attempt made against their liberty. The French, who by fubfidies, and that fpirit of intrigue which diftinguifh their minifters in every court, laid hold of this occafion, to make the Swedes declare againft his Pruffian majefty. The war, however, being undertaken againft the will of the king, was profecuted without vigour, and they therefore embraced the firft opportunity of concluding a peace, which they never ought to have broke. The Swedes muft keep a watchful eye on the Ruffians, who aim at further conquefts on the Baltick: this cannot be executed, without endangering the fafety of Sweden. Pruffia and Denmark have a common intereft in oppofing the progrefs of the Ruffians. How impolitick therefore were the Swedes to have acted on quite contrary principles. Had the confederacy fucceeded againft Pruffia, Sweden and Denmark, particularly the former, would have been the victims of their bad policy, and fell an eafy prey to the ambition of Ruffia.

A

MILITARY DESCRIPTION

OF THE

SEAT of WAR.

Of BOHEMIA and MORAVIA.

THESE two great provinces belong to the emprefs of Germany. They are feparated from Silefia, Lufatia, Saxony, and part of Bavaria, and Auftria, by a continued chain of very high mountains, which neceffarily renders the communication between thofe countries very difficult, there being very few military roads [a]. The firft of thefe goes from Olmutz, in Moravia, to a town called Sternberg, and there divides itfelf into two; the one goes by Hoff to Troppau, and Jägerndorff, in the Auftrian Silefia; the other paffes by Friedland, Wurbenthal, and Zuckmantel, and from thence goes to Neifs. Thefe two roads, particularly the laft, may be confidered as one continual defile, formed by the mountains, ravins, rivers, &c. and therefore may, no doubt, be defended by a few troops, if properly placed, againft a numerous army. The Pruffians have indeed one very great advantage: they can, by fending two corps, the one by Jägerndorff, and the other, out of the

---

[a] A road where infantry, cavalry, heavy artillery, and all kind of carriages can pafs.

county

county of Glatz, from Habelſchwert towards Altſtat, and Schonberg, force the Auſtrians to quit any poſition they may take, between Freudenthal and Neiſs, by cutting off their communication with Olmutz, from whence they muſt neceſſarily draw their ſubſiſtence. Whereas theſe can take no central poſition, that will effectually hinder the Pruſſians from entering Moravia, by the way of Zuckmantel, from the county of Glatz, and by Troppau, and unite theſe three columns with ſafety; Olmutz being too far back, can be of no uſe to guard the paſſages beween Moravia and Sileſia.

As the king of Pruſſia cannot from any place, more conveniently, carry on the war againſt the empreſs's dominions, than from Neiſs, into Moravia, nor where his ſucceſſes would be attended with more fatal conſequences; it is ſurpriſing her majeſty has not thought proper to oppoſe, on that ſide, a ſtronger barrier than Olmutz, which is certainly a very indifferent place. The fine defence general Marſhal made, during the laſt war, was owing as much to the weakneſs of the Pruſſian army, as to his own talents and vigilance, as will evidently appear by the hiſtory of that famous ſiege. This fortreſs is ſo far back, that it leaves all the avenues leading from Sileſia and Glatz, into Moravia, quite open, and a conſiderable body of men cannot be ſent far into the mountains, without evident riſk: nothing would be more efficacious to check the Pruſſians, than the building a fortreſs, either in the neighbourhood of Alſtadt, or between, Freudenthal and Zuckmantel; or laſtly, between Jägerndorff, and Johanniſthal. The firſt, would be a check on Glatz and Neiſs, at the ſame time, and enable the Auſtrians to make continual incurſions into thoſe two provinces, without any riſk: nor does it appear poſſible for the Pruſſians to penetrate into Moravia, either from Glatz or Neiſs, without previouſly taking this

fortreſs

fortrefs; becaufe a corps of troops pofted here, and fuftained by a ftrong garrifon, would cut off all communication with thofe two places, and foon force an army that would advance towards Olmutz, to fall back or perifh.

The fecond and third, would, indeed, effectually hinder the Pruffians from advancing into Moravia, 'till they had taken them: but the fiege of them would be more eafy, becaufe fuch a body of troops might be fent from upper Silefia, and from Glatz, to feize the defiles between them, and Moravia, as would make it impoffible to relieve them.

Moft men think that a camp, or fortrefs, is well placed, if they cannot be approached without great difficulty, which is true only, in cafe they have in themfelves all the refources neceffary for their defence; but as that feldom or ever happens, the perfection of the one and the other would be, to find a fituation that prefents to the enemy all the difficulties poffible; and which, at the fame time, may be eafily fuccoured, if neceffary. The difficulty to find fuch a fituation, or the want of that fure, coup d'œil, has determined many engineers, to choofe the plains for their fortreffes, which frees them from the cenfure of having ill chofe their ground, and flatters their vanity, by giving them an opportunity, to produce all the different works they have feen in the fchools, and make fuch a fine appearance on paper.

Another road goes from Olmutz, by Litau and Alftadt, into the county of Glatz. The next principal road, is that, which goes from the circle of Königfgratz, by Neuftat and Nachod, into the county of Glatz, and from thence into the other provinces of Silefia: it is not lefs difficult than the others above-mentioned, being like them, one continual defile, particularly, when it enters the Pruffian dominions, where it is almoft impoffible for a confiderable body of troops to march, if they meet with any refiftance; efpecially, in going

from

from Bohemia towards Glatz, as the mountains rife gradually; from whence appears, that the Pruffians can with more eafe penetrate into Bohemia, than the Auftrians can, into the county of Glatz. The firft have another confiderable advantage; they can be provided with every thing from the fortrefs of Glatz, which gives them a fafe retreat, when pufhed back by fuperior forces: they are mafters of the avenues which lead into Bohemia; which, being intirely open and fruitful, they can enter with eafe, and fubfift for a confiderable time; whereas the Auftrians cannot enter the country of Glatz at all, if the paffes are properly guarded, and even fhould they force back the pofts placed in them, they can find no fubfiftence in the country, and muft begin their operations by the fiege of Glatz, which, from its very advantageous fituation, can fcarce be taken, though left to the defence of its own garrifon, and certainly not at all, if there is a confiderable body of troops in the country to fuftain it.

The hiftory of the laft and preceding wars, confirms what is here advanced. In the firft, it was reduced by famine, and, in the laft, chance, cowardice, and ignorance, of all which, general Laudhon took proper advantages, were the immediate caufes of its being taken.

The next road goes likewife from the circle of Konigfgratz, by Trautenau and Landfhut, to Schweidnitz, and Jauer, in Silefia. This, like the others, is a continual defile, and fo difficult, that when the paffes are properly guarded, no army can penetrate into Silefia, on this fide. The Pruffians have a fine pofition near Landfhut, from whence they may, by an eafy march on the left, cover the road that goes from Friedland to Schweïdnitz, and fuftain effectually any corps, they may fend to Schmidberg and Hirfchberg. It was from this camp that Fouquet, with an inconfiderable army, fo

often

often baffled the attempts made by the Auftrians, though much fuperior, to penetrate that way into Silefia, and was at laft overpowered, and intirely defeated in it, by his own fault.

The Pruffians have here the fame advantages as on the fide of Glatz. The fortrefs of Schweidnitz, being another place of arms, fupplys them with every thing they want; and being fo near, enables them to begin their operations, much fooner than the Auftrians. The mountains are filled with villages, where an army may be put in cantonments with fafety, if care is taken to occupy the defiles, between them and Bohemia, which they can do with eafe, being within the Pruffian dominions: nothing therefore, can hinder them from invading that province on this fide, even if the Auftrians had an army there; becaufe that army cannot take any pofition nearer the avenues that lead into it; than behind the Elbe, fome where between Konigfhoff and Königfgraatz, which can, effectually, hinder the Pruffians from advancing any farther; but cannot prevent their entring it.

When one confiders that the Pruffians muft, from the fituation of their country, make their chief efforts on this fide, as well, becaufe they can penetrate with fafety in various columns, can be fupplied, abundantly, from Glatz and Schweidnitz, with provifions, ftores, &c. and can retire without danger in cafe of misfortune, one is amazed, to fee her majefty leave this province, entirely, defencelefs, and expofed to the continual ravages of the enemy. As there is no kind of fortrefs, nothing lefs than an army, can defend it againft the incurfions, that may be made from the county of Glatz, and from the mountains of Landfhut.

If the enemy once paffes the Elbe, above Konigfgratz, all the provinces on the right of that river, muft be abandoned; the troops pofted on the frontiers of Lufatia, muft inftantly, fall back to Prague, for fear of being cut off. Even the army itself must fall back into the circle of Chrudim, in order to cover Moravia, and keep open the communication with Auſtria and the Danube. Whereas, if a fortreſs capable of containing 10,000 foot and 4000 horſe, was placed behind the Elbe, between Königſhoff, and Konig(gratz, with caſerns and magazines vaulted, bomb-proof, the Pruſſians, could not take it, without infinite trouble; and it would certainly hold out ſome months, if we judge by their ſkill, on other occaſions, and give time, to come to its relief. This ſituation is ſo advantageous, that it not only covers the country on that ſide, but likewiſe facilitates the means of entring Sileſia. As it may be made a general place of arms, to ſupply the armies deſtined on that ſide, nor can the enemy leave it behind him and penetrate into the country, becauſe the garriſon alone, with ſome croats and huſſars, would cut off his communication with Sileſia and Glatz, in ſuch a manner, as would ſoon force him to retire, or make him, and his army periſh, though he ſhould leave a corps of 20,000 men, to obſerve the place, to ſecure his convoys.

Beſides, a fortreſs of that kind, and a numerous garriſon, muſt force the enemy to keep a conſiderable corps, both in the county of Glatz, and in the mountains of Landſhut. The advantages of ſuch a fortreſs, are infinite, and in my opinion, renders it abſolutely neceſſary.

The next road goes from the circle of Buntzlau, by Bakhofen, Swigan, Libenau, Riechenberg, where it divides into two; the one goes to Friedland, and thence towards Grieffenberg, in Sileſia, Seidenberg, in Luſatia. This road paſſes likewiſe through many very high mountains; and therefore not eaſily to be paſſed, if there are troops to defend the defiles.

Though the king of Pruſſia, will never make his chief effort on
this

this side, having no place of arms, at a proper distance, yet as in every war with the Austrians, he will think it necessary to occupy Saxony, some division of his army will always enter Bohemia, on the side of Lusatia, while it remains quite open as at present: wherefore it would, no doubt, be very proper, to have as near the frontiers as possible, some considerable fortress, which a division of twenty thousand men, can neither suddenly take, nor safely leave behind them, nor could any troops take their winter quarters, any where in the mountains, from Friedland to Schandau, or even at Grieffenberg, Marklissa, Lauban, and Gorlitz, if a considerable fortress is placed in the neighbourhood of Friedland: neither can the communication be kept up between Silesia and Saxony, unless an army be posted to secure it. To these great and obvious reasons may be added, that as Silesia, is quite an open country, without any fortress to cover it, from Marklissa to Crossen, near Frankfort, it might be attacked, on that side rather, than on that of Moravia, and Bohemia, which now can't be done, without leaving an army to cover these two provinces. But if they are secured, by the fortresses proposed to be made in Moravia, and near Konigsgratz; the Austrians might, we think, enter Silesia, by the way of Lusatia, provided they have a place of arms, near Friedland, which would enable them, as we think, to act with safety and vigour on that side. The want of it, rendered ineffectual, the victories gained by the Russians at Zullichau, and Cunnersdorff, and every attempt, the Austrians made, on the Queiss, and Bober.

Should the different fortresses, above proposed, be executed, 30,000 men, besides their garrisons, will, it's thought, be more than sufficient to cover Bohemia, all the remainder of her majesty's forces, may then, act with success on the Queiss, and Bober, otherwise not.

The next road goes likewise from the circle of Buntzlau, by

Leypa,

Leypa, and Gabel, to Zittau, in Lufatia: this is the leaſt difficult of any as yet defcribed. In the mountains, however, about Gabel, there are fome defiles, which may eafily be guarded, with few troops.

The next road goes from the fame province, by Rumburg, and from thence tawards Löbau, in Lufatia. This is extreemly difficult, and, during the courfe of the war, I do not remember it was taken by any confiderable corps, excepting by that of the prince of Pruffia, after the battle of Kollin. Little ufe can be made of thefe two laſt roads, by the Pruffians, being fo far from their depots, excepting for fome divfion of their army, when they propofe invading Bohemia on different fides at the fame time, and therefore it feems ufelefs, to fortify them.

The next, and one of the moſt important roads, in all this country, is that which goes from Prague, by Budyn, Lowofitz, Auffig, Peterfwald, and Ghiſhubel, where it enters Saxony. This road is one continual defile, from Lowofitz to the laſt mentioned place, runs clofe to the Elbe, from Lowofitz to Auffig, where the river Bila cuts it, another deep ravin beyond Peterfwald; and a third at Ghiſhubel. In each of thefe three places, are fuch advantageous pofitions, that twelve or fourteen battalions, would be able to defend them againſt an army, though there be no kind of fortrefs, and if there was a good one, it would be fcarce pofiible to invade Bohemia, on the fide of Saxony, with fuccefs. Whenever an army propofes pafling from the one country into the other, it is abfolutely neceffary to be mafters of the Elbe, becaufe it is by that river alone, fuch armies muſt fubfiſt, the mountains being fo high, and the roads fo bad, that for many months in the year, no carriage can pafs; a fortrefs therefore here, would be an invincible obſtacle for an army coming from either country.

The next road goes likewife from the plains of Lowofitz,

over

over the mountains by Töplitz, and from thence by Zinwalde, into Saxony. This road is very bad, and so full of defiles, that it is scarce fit for any but infantry: there are many positions to be taken on it, the principal one is near Toplitz.

The next goes out of the circle of Saatz, by Laun, and Commotau, and from thence over the Basberg into Saxony. This and the next which goes likewise from the circle of Saatz, by Caaden, over the Kupferberg, into Saxony, are extreamly difficult, and when the defiles have been properly guarded the Prussians have always been repulsed. During the war, excepting in 1757, when prince Maurice passed there in two columns. Scarce any thing but light troops ever attempted passing these defiles.

From the circle of Ellenbogen, there go two roads, the one over the mountains to Plauen, and the other through Egra. Both these, are in some measure impassable, for an army coming into Bohemia, because it would not be safe to pass through such great defiles, so near a fortress. These are the principal roads and passes, which occur, in the counties where the war was carried on in that part of Germany.

Bohemia and Moravia are watered by many rivers, the principal of which are the Teifs, which rises in the mountains of Silesia, called Schneeberg, and runs by Alstadt, Muglitz, Littau, Olmutz, Hradisch, &c. and falls into the Danube, at Presburg; in the latter part of its course, it is called the Morava: it is not navigable, nor can any position be taken on its banks, to stop an enemy coming from Silesia. The best, however, is on the heights about Littau with the right extending towards Olmutz, and a corps further on towards Muglitz, otherwise a column coming down the Teifs would render that position very hazardous.

dous. This is, no doubt, the moſt proper poſition of any to cover Olmutz, which cannot be attacked while an army is here, nor can it well be forced, by any indirect manœuvre to quit it, being ſupplied with proviſions from Olmutz, nor can an enemy advance towards Auſtria, leaving that fortreſs, and army behind him.

There are many more, ſmall, rivers between Olmutz and Brinn, which, paſſing through the mountains, furniſh every where excellent camps. Moravia, in general, is a very ſtrong country, and may be defended by a ſmall army againſt a very numerous one, as appeared in the war which happened after the death of Charles the VIth. For then prince Charles, aided by the great Kevenhuller, at the head of a very inconſiderable body of troops, compared with thoſe of the enemies, drove them intirely out of that country, and Bohemia, merely by the ſuperiority of manœuvres, which the face of the country permitted him to execute.

The Elbe riſes in the mountains of Sileſia, called the Rieſengebürg, and runs by Arnau, Kònigſhoff, Jaromitz, Kònigſgratz, Pardubitz, Neuhoff, Kollin, Nimburg, Brandeiſs, where the Iſer falls into it, Melnick, where the Moldau comes into it, Leütmeritz, above which, the Egra falls into it, Auſſig, and from thence to Kònigſtein in Saxony, it is navigable only as far as Lowoſitz, where it grows conſiderable. In all this extenſive courſe few good poſitions can be taken on its banks. The firſt and moſt important of any upon it, and indeed in the whole country, is between Konigſhoff, and Kònigſgratz, from whence an army can effectually hinder an enemy coming from Schweidnitz and Glatz, from penetrating into the interior parts of Bohemia.

There

There are other positions to be taken, between Nimburg, and Brandeifs, which cover Prague againft an army coming from Lufatia. Between thefe places and Saxony, no pofition can be taken on its banks, becaufe it runs paralel, to the road that pafs from the one country into the other; fo that only the right or left wing of an army camped between Lowofitz and Aufig, can be pofted on it, according as the front is placed.

On the Zaffava, one pofition only of confequence can be taken, and that at Benefchau, from whence you may cover the two great roads that lead from Prague to Vienna.

The Moldau, on which fome pofitions may be taken, which cover Bohemia, Upper and Lower Auftria, in cafe any attempt be made from Voigtland, in Saxony: It was from thefe pofitions that the French, under marfhal Maillebois, were effectually prevented from penetrating into Bohemia, and relieving marfhal Belleifle, then befieged in Prague.

This is the ftrongeft place on the river; and indeed in the whole country, and is well fortified; but being commanded by the neighbouring hills, very extenfive, and divided by the Moldau, it requires fuch an immenfe quantity of ftores and artillery, and fuch a numerous garrifon, that it feems doubtful whether any attempt fhould be made to defend it or not, excepting by a couple of battalions, meerly to protect it, from plunder, by capitulating. The fate of this city, in the war of 1741, fhews the truth of this opinion. The firft time, it was taken by affault, with a garrifon of near 4000 men in it; the fecond time, it refifted a very few days only; and the third, it was abandoned precipitately by the Pruffians, on their quitting Bohemia. In this laft war, its fate would have been decided in a few days more, and it would have been taken with an army in it.

The

The Egra rifes in the circle of that name, and runs by the town of Egra, thence by Ellenbogen, Saatz, Laun, and Budyn; and a little way from this laſt town it falls into the Elbe. The only town of ſtrength on this river is Egra, which is well fortified; but being commanded by a hill, on the left of the river, it cannot make any long defence; and therefore in the laſt war, it was debated, whether it ſhould be diſmantled, or not.

It is remarkable, that, in general, the banks on the right of this river are higheſt; and conſequently furniſh eaſy means for its defence. There are many good poſitions to be taken on it; the firſt and principal however is, that, on the right of the river behind Budyn, by which an enemy, coming from Saxony, by the way of Auſſig, (which, as we have ſaid, is the principal debouché into Bohemia) may be effectually ſtopped, if another ſtrong corps is placed higher up, towards Laun, which at the ſame time ſtops any column coming by the way of Commotau. This body of troops muſt be ſtrong enough to diſpute the paſſage, 'till the army poſted at Budyn has time to come up, which may be done by an eaſy march on the left; and if in 1756 the duke of Aremberg's corps had taken this poſition, inſtead of falling back to Mickovitz, the king of Pruſſia would have found it difficult to paſs the Egra, and probably would have failed in the attempt, as Gen. Brown could have oppoſed him with a very numerous army.

This country, like moſt others in Europe, was formerly governed by the feudal ſyſtem; it is ſtill ſo, in ſome meaſure, and notwithſtanding the vaſt power of the houſe of Auſtria, the nobility have ſome privileges: for theſe reaſons there is an infinite number of towns fortified, or rather ſurrounded with an old wall, after the Gothic manner, whoſe uſe is very great

and

and extensive, as they furnish effectual means to carry on the *petite guerre* with success, and consequently harrass an enemy extremely, by rendering his convoys and subsistence precarious, which at last must force him to abandon the interior part of the country, and approach the frontiers. They likewise enable you, with a small army, to dispute every inch of ground with your enemy, who will not presume to separate his troops 'till he has forced you back on the Danube. For this reason, the Prussians, French, and Saxons, in the war of 1741, though they were soon masters of it, on the appearance of any small army against them, they were obliged to abandon it; and indeed we don't think it can be preserved, if conquered, unless you include Moravia and Austria, as far as the Danube; then indeed, having this great river for a barrier, it may be kept, otherwise not.

Though the country, from what we have said, will appear strong, and is really so; it has, however, many inconveniencies, which make it impossible to hinder an invasion, particularly on the side of Silesia. The mountains, which separate these two countries, make a part of Silesia, and therefore belong to the king of Prussia, who is thereby master of the defiles, near which, he has the fortresses of Neifs, Glatz, and Schweidnitz, where he can, with ease and secrefy, make the necessary preparations; and in one march, he may enter Bohemia in three different columns, which nothing in the world can prevent, as no position can be taken near enough to the Debouchés, to prevent his subsisting, and encamping so advantageously, between your army and the mountains, that you cannot force him to repass them. The nearest and best positions that can be taken to cover the country from an invasion, on the side of Schweidnitz and Glatz, are those already mentioned, behind the Elbe, at Königshoff and Königsgratz, which, however, you must abandon, unless you are strong enough to hinder him from entering Moravia on your right, by the way of Zuckmantel, as it happened in the campaign of 1758, and out of Bohemia on your left by Friedland and Gabel. If you fail in this, you must instantly fall back into Moravia, to cover Vienna; or to the Moldau, to cover Prague. In the interior part of the country, the best position, without doubt, is that in the neighbourhood of Collin and Czaslau, as you may from thence, in a few marches, be either behind the Elbe at Königsgratz, approach the Moldau, or fall back into Moravia, as the case may require.

The positions to be taken in that part of the country, are those of Lëutomischel, Müglitz, Littau, with strong corps towards Zuckmantel and Troppau, to cover the debouchés on that side, where they are securely posted, and can be attacked only in front: in which case they fall back on your army, or on Olmutz. By taking either of these positions you cover Moravia and Austria, and have your communication open with Bohemia, where no enemy dare separate, while you are in force in Moravia. Another great inconveniency in the defence of this country, is, that no considerable magazines can with safety be placed, any where, but at Prague or Olmutz, which are too far back from the frontiers, and your army must be supplied from thence by land carriage, a thing very difficult at the end of a campaign, particularly if the war continues long in the country, and makes horses and oxen scarce.

This

Of SILESIA and the County of GLATZ.

THIS country lies from south to south-east of Bohemia. It extends in length from Liebenau, on the frontiers of Brandeburg, to Upper Silesia, on the frontiers of Poland and Hungary, near 240 miles. Its breadth, including the county of Glatz, to Millitsch, on the frontiers of Poland, is near 120 miles. It is peopled, by near a million and a half of inhabitants, and produces an yearly avenue of about four millions of dollars, and is one of the most fruitful and richest provinces in Europe.

It has been already said, that it is separated from Bohemia, by a chain of mountains, running from Zuckmantel, on the frontiers of Moravia, to Greiffenberg on the river Queiss. From Lusace, it is separated by this river, which runs by Greiffenberg, Marklissa, and Lauban, and falls at Halbau into the Bober. This last river serves as a barrier, on the side of Upper Lusace, 'till it falls into the Oder at Crossen.

The advantageous situation of this country, enables the king of Prussia to invade Bohemia with facility and success: whereas any attempt from Bohemia against Silesia would be attended with much danger and difficulty. A small army posted, any where, in the neighbourhood of Glatz, with two corps; the one between Freywald and Johansthal, and the other about Trautenau, would, I am persuaded, render any attempts against it, vain and fruitless. An army so posted cannot be forced by any direct manœuvre, because the country is extremely strong, and it might retire under the cannon of Glatz: and though either of the two corps posted, as we suppose, on the right and left, were pushed back; you could not presume to advance into Silesia with an army, leaving the enemy in the county of Glatz; because from thence, he could cut off your communication both with Bohemia and Moravia; and consequently, in a few days, would force you to fall back into these countries, or perish in the mountains, as the country between these mountains and the fortresses of Neiss and Schweidnitz, could not supply an army for two days only. Much less could you attempt any thing against these places, if there be any troops in the county of Glatz; or any corps, however inconsiderable, in the neighbourhood of them, your army must subsist from your magazines in Bohemia, which you cannot possibly bring into Silesia, while the enemy is in force in the county of Glatz. And though there be no enemy there, your transports, however numerous, are soon wore out, particularly if any rain falls, which makes the roads absolutely impassable. Then you must not think of bringing up your heavy artillery, ammunitions, &c. till the place is entirely invested, and you have formed a considerable magazine near your camp. Such preparations require much more time than is necessary, to enable the king to come to its relief. Hence it appears, how difficult, the conquest of Silesia must be, while there is any small army to cover it. The progress of the Austrians in the campaigns of 1757, 1760, and 1761, was, we think, intirely owing to the bad conduct of the Prussian generals; which we shall demonstrate when we give an account of those campaigns.

This country is watered by small rivers, and, like Bohemia, is covered with woods, and intersected with hills and valleys: and consequently furnishes, every where, excellent camps. The chief positions on this side, are those in the neighbourhood of Glatz, at Frankenstein, Wartha, &c. of which we have given an account. On the left is one near Otmoschau, which covers
Neiss.

in GERMANY.

Neifs: on the right is that of Landfhut, which covers Schweidnitz. There is another on the heights of Wûrben, between Schweidnitz and Breflau, which covers both: another, behind the Reichenbachifch Waffer, with the right at Púltzen, and the left at Faulebrucken, which anfwers the fame purpofe: another between Liebenthal and Löwenberg, which is excellent, and covers the country effectually againft an army advancing by the way of Görlîtz, Markliffa, and Lauban.

Further down the Queifs, is a good camp between Naumburg and Buntzlau, but it fhould not be occupied, except in fome very particular cafe; as the enemy could pafs the Queifs, and enter Silefia on your left, by Lauban; near which is a very good camp for a fmall corps to ferve as a vanguard to the army pofted at Löwenberg. Still further down, on the Bober, is a good camp at Sagan, and at Chriftianftadt, which covers that fide effectually.

The only navigable river in this country is the Oder, which rifes in the mountains of Hungary, not far from Jablunka. It runs by Rattibor, Kofel, Oppelen, Tefchen, Brieg, Breflau, Grofs Glogau, Frankfort, Cuftrin, and Stettin, a little below which it falls into the Baltic.

The firft place of any ftrength you meet with, on this river, is Kofel, which, though very fmall, is ftrong by its fituation, and could it contain a numerous garrifon, would be a refpectable bulwark againft the Auftrians and Hungarians. The other places we have named, as far as Breflau, are of no other ufe, than to cover the country againft the incurfions of light troops, and to form magazines, and fecure the fruits of the earth in cafe of a war.

Breflau,

Breslau, the capital of Silesia, is a large and well-peopled town; but though pretty well fortified, is not capable of making any considerable defence; because it is commanded by a neighbouring height: it has no out-works of consequence. Besides, great part of the town or suburbs are without the wall; under the cover of which, you may begin your approaches very near; and the ditch not being protected by a good glacis, and a well-pallisaded covered-way, you may get into the town in a very short time. 'Tis however, in other respects, of great use; as you may with safety form there magazines of provisions and stores: and you may lodge there a good body of troops to recover themselves during the winter quarters. It may likewise cover a camp, if the ground is well chosen. Its garrison, when left to itself, ought to be numerous, in order to protect the country. From Breslau, still following the course of the river, you come to Grofs Glogau, which may justly be esteemed the key and bulwark of Lower Silesia. It is a strong fortress, when compared with those of this country, though nothing at all compared with those in Flanders.

There are generally immense magazines, and a numerous garrison in this town. It covers the country so effectually, that no enterprise of consequence can be undertaken on that side of Silesia, until you are master of it. The taking of it will be no easy matter, as the king will always have an army in this neighbourhood, to observe an enemy coming from Poland, and if it be too weak to keep the field, it will find a secure retreat under the cannon of this fortress, from whence it cannot be forced by any direct manœuvre. Should the enemy attempt to leave you behind, and march to Breslau, you can be there before him; or by sending a body of hussars into Poland, cut

off

off his subsistences so effectually, as to force him immediately to abandon his designs and return to the frontiers of that country: and as the king takes care to have all the corn of the country deposited at Breslau and Glogau, the enemy finds nothing but the growing crop, on which no army can subsist a day; particularly in that part of the country bordering on the Oder, which is generally sandy, and therefore by no means fruitful. From hence it appears, that an army coming from Poland cannot, however numerous, undertake any thing solid. No magazine can be formed nearer the frontiers of Silesia, than at Posen, sixty miles from Glogau. Such a magazine, however abundant, can scarcely supply the daily consumption of a numerous army, while it remains in that neighbourhood, much less can it be transported to Glogau, and supply the army there for at least two months. How can the heavy artillery, an immense quantity of stores necessary for such a siege, be brought there? How, therefore, undertake it? even supposing, what probably will never happen, that it be left to the defence of a common garrison, and that there be no army to cover it. This shews why the Russians could not, for want of a sufficient magazine at Posen, approach the frontiers of Silesia till the month of July: and then their operations were chiefly regulated by the necessity of making the army subsist, rather than with a view to any military enterprise. As they could not subsist in any one place, long enough, to think of undertaking any thing of consequence; they were, notwithstanding their repeated victories, obliged in the month of october, to abandon a country, which their own ravages, and the nature of the circumstances, had rendered incapable of supporting them during the winter. They must necessarily fall back on the Lower Vistula, where

they

they have their magazines. For these reasons, all the operations of this army were reduced to marching from the Vistula into Silesia, and after fighting and ravaging the country, to the returning again on the Vistula.

We shall conclude this description of Silesia with observing, that the greatest advantage arising from the favourable situation, and nature of this country, in our opinion, consists in this: that the king, covered with the places of Silesia, is enabled to make all his motions with safety and celerity; that his armies are abundantly supplied, on the spot where they encamp; that a small corps, protected by these places, supply the place of a great army, and that so effectually, that nothing of consequence, can be undertaken in that country while they exist. Whoever considers attentively what we have said on this subject, will probably feel his admiration for the king of Prussia, and his contempt for the Austrian and Russian generals, considerably diminished.

Further down the Oder, in the marquisate of Brandeburg, lies the city of Francfort, a rich and populous place. It is of no other use, however, when considered in a military view, than to cover magazines, which you must form here, and at Crossen, for an army you may send on the Warta towards Posen, and those parts of Poland.

Further down, at the confluent of the Warta into the Oder, is Custrin. This place is small, and not at all strong, yet the Russians, who attacked it in 1758, failed in their attempt. It held out till the king came and relieved it, by gaining the battle of Zorndorff. This confirms what we have said of the difficulties, attending such an enterprise, as the siege of Glogau, or indeed of any place of considerable strength, unless you can form your magazines near such places, or that the country itself should be able

to

to supply your army. But this can never happen as to ammunitions and stores, nor even as to subsistences; if care is taken to make the farmers deposit their grain in those places, where a siege is expected.

The situation of Custrin is very advantageous, and may be considered as one of the chief keys of Silesia and Brandeburg, particularly the last, whenever an invasion is expected from the Lower Vistula, that is, from Warsaw to Dantzig.

Some one column must pass here, and it would be no ways safe to penetrate into Brandeburg, without having previously taken Custrin and Stettin. It were to be wished, that some means could be found to augment the fortifications of the former, so as to make it capable of holding a numerous garrison of horse and foot. This would add infinitely to its importance, and it would then effectually cover the country on that side. Stettin, from its situation chiefly, is capable of a long defence, as appeared when it was taken from the Swedes, in the beginning of this century. It is of infinite consequence to the king of Prussia, as it covers Brandeburg and Pomerania, in such a manner, that though these provinces may be overrun and ravaged, they can never be conquered: and we doubt whether any of those powers, who may hereafter have views on this town, will be in a condition to take it, without having made a couple of successful campaigns, there being so many things to be done previous to the siege of such a place.

Colberg is on the sea coast, and though many miles distant from Stettin, it may be considered as an outwork to that place, it being the only post in that neighbourhood, where magazines may be formed to besiege that fortress. No considerable supply of provisions can be got, from the produces of the country:

it must

it muſt be brought from Livonia, Finland, Sweden, &c. by ſea. So muſt the artillery, ammunitions, and ſtores, which cannot be tranſported from the Viſtula by land. Hence it appears of what conſequence Colberg is; and we are therefore much ſurpriſed, that the king of Pruſſia ſhould have neglected this place. Its fortifications are ſmall and inſignificant beyond conception, and could not, if properly attacked, have held out two days. The defence it made redounds as much to the honour of the governor, as it does the imputation of ignorance on the beſiegers.

If this place was made fit to hold a garriſon of 4000 foot, and 2000 horſe, we think it would be impregnable to a Ruſſian army; as they could ſcarce ever be provided with the neceſſary means to reduce it. Beſides, it would effectually ſtop the progreſs of an army coming that way; eſpecially if Cuſtrin was likewiſe put in the ſituation we have mentioned. Glogau, Cuſtrin, Colberg, and Stettin, may be rendered inſuperable barriers, on this ſide the Pruſſian dominions; as Neiſs, Glatz, and Schweidnitz, are on the other. The putting theſe places in a reſpectable condition, is the more neceſſary, as Pomerania and Brandeburg are open on that ſide, and have abſolutely no interior defence.

The frontiers of Pomerania, towards the Swedes and Mecklenburgers, are ſtrong by nature, and do not require the help of art; as the Pruſſians are too powerful to fear any thing from that quarter.

Of Pruſſia I ſhall only ſay, it cannot be effectually defended while it depends on the houſe of Brandeburg; becauſe thoſe who attack it are borderers, and have therefore at hand all the means that can inſure ſucceſs, and all the reſources neceſſary to

rcover

recover themselves after a defeat: whereas those who are to defend it, are deprived of every advantage, and were they subject to no other loss, than what naturally attends war, in one campaign, they would be reduced to the necessity of abandoning it, as they could not possibly be recruited in time, receive horses for remounting their cavalry, or be supplied with stores, &c. we are therefore surprised his majesty should attempt to defend it: He, probably, held the Russians in such contempt, that he did not doubt of their being easily beaten, and forced back into their own country. But he saw his error, and therefore, after his first campaign, abandoned the country. Could his majesty change this country with the Poles for that on the Lower Vistula, it would be much for his advantage. I shall dwell longer on the subject of defending a distant country, when I examine the war in Westphalia and Portugal, independent of politics, and merely in a military view.

To the left of Pomerania, the king has the strong fortress of Magdeburg on the Elbe, a place of great strength, and of equal importance; as he may form there in twenty-four hours, such a body of troops, as will keep in awe the Saxons on the one side, and Holstein, Mecklenburg, and Hanover on the other. As to the king's dominions on the Rhine, we rather think there should be no fortress: because it would be almost impossible to defend them against an enemy who is on that frontier: and it would be too difficult to wrest them from him, should he become master of them: whereas, if left open, he will be obliged to abandon them.

The fate of Wesel in this last war confirms our opinion.

Of SAXONY and LUSACE.

IN speaking of Bohemia and Silesia, we have already said, that the first is separated from Saxony by a chain of mountains running from Egra to Pirna, and from Lusace by the same chain of mountains running from Pirna to Friedland. From this place, Lusace is separated from Silesia, by the Queifs and Bober. In all this, so extensive, frontier, nor indeed on that towards Brandeburg and Thuringue, can any position be taken, by any army the elector of Saxony can raise, so as to cover his country effectually, because it is not strong, either by art, or nature. However, to preserve the capital from an enemy, coming by the way of Aussig from Bohemia, a camp may be taken behind the ravin of Ghishubel, or further back at Grofs Zedlitz: this indeed is a resource for a few days only, because the enemy, by marching a column on the right of the Elbe by Schandau, may come and encamp on the heights near the Weissenhirsch, from whence he will soon destroy Dresden, or force you to a composition: still more useless would any camp in Lusace be, because you can from no one place there, cover that country, or any part of Saxony, either towards Bohemia, or on the side of Brandeburg and lower Saxony.

The situation of the Prussian dominions enables his majesty to form different points of attack from Magdeburg, Brandeburg, and Silesia, and his being so much superior to the elector of Saxony, would render all the efforts of that prince in the defence of his country vain. It is an unhappy situation; but such it is.

Saxony

Saxony alone cannot withstand either Prussia or Austria; and therefore, by force, or persuasion, must be made a party in every war between these contending rivals. And as the country is intirely open on the side of Prussia, he can over-run it and be at the capital, before it is possible for the Austrians to bring an army to cover it. We think, therefore, that Saxony should unite herself to the house of Brandeburg. In the beginning of the war, which happened at the death of Charles the sixth, Saxony was connected with Prussia, and certainly suffered nothing from this connection; and had she not altered her system, it is my opinion she might have reaped some advantages from this union. In the last part of that war, she was united with Austria, and was the victim of it. In a few days, Saxony was lost, and could not be recovered, but by the mediation of England, and on such terms as the victor thought proper to impose.

The transactions of this last war confirm our opinion, and shews the absolute necessity of changing her political system. She must forget that she has been equal to the house of Brandeburg: her jealousy must give way to sentiments of self-preservation, which we think can be insured only by entering into strong and close connections with Prussia.

The interior of this country is intersected by many small rivers, and by an infinite number of ravins, generally so deep, that they are almost impassable. Parallel to the Elbe runs the Mulda; it rises in the mountains called the Ertzgeburg, and it falls into the Elbe, near Dessau. Its farthest distance from the Elbe, is about twelve miles: though it is no where very deep, yet as it runs through a deep ravin, whose banks are very high

high and craggy, it is impossible to pass it, if you meet with the least opposition.

Between this river and the Elbe, are many good camps, but no one position that can effectually cover the capital.

The first camp is on the right of the Weistritz, with the right wing at Plauen, and the left, on the mountain by Potchapel. To make this camp secure, you must have a strong corps on the other side of the ravin by Posendorff, between Rabenau and Dippoldiswalda, to cover your flank and watch Friberg. The enemy coming up the Elbe may encamp with safety, on the heights of Kesselsdorff.

The second camp is further down the Elbe, with the right at Monzig, and the left at Rothschönberg, with a deep ravin in front, through which runs a marshy rivulet.

On the other side of this ravin, is another excellent camp, called the Kattsenhauser, which the Prussians have often occupied during the war. They likewise occupied one near Meissen; which was as bad as possible, as will be evident, when we come to give an account of some actions which have passed there, during the war.

The third is at Lomatch. The fourth is at Ochatz, which may be made very strong, by throwing up some few redoubts before the center, and beyond the right.

The fifth is at Strehlen, which is good, whichever way it is taken; but you must have a corps at Hubertzburg.

The last of any consequence is at Torgau; which is a good one whatever way you place your front. However strong these camps may be in front, no army can remain long in them, if they are not secured by strong corps, on the left side of the Mulda, and on the right of the Elbe; but if this precaution is neglected, an army, for example, destined to cover Dresden

and

and Bohemia, muſt inſtantly fall back on that town, to ſecure its communication with Bohemia, if the enemy ſends a corps, beyond the Mulda or the Elbe. The ſame thing will happen to an army coming up that river; a corps poſted beyond thoſe rivers will ſoon force him back to ſecure his communication with the Lower Elbe, and with Brandeburg. This will be confirmed by the operations of the war in that country.

Having explained the views of the different powers at war, and given a proper deſcription of the country, wherein it was proſecuted. We ſhall now proceed to give an account of its various operations, hoping to make it an uſeful, and agreeable work to all military men; for whoſe uſe it was chiefly undertaken.

HISTORY

HISTORY

OF THE

WAR in GERMANY.

CAMPAIGN of 1756.

THE king of Pruſſia attempted to enter into a negotiation with the court of Vienna, and by that means gain time, by which he hoped to find ſome methods of diſſolving the confederacy; or at leaſt to prevent its immediate effect. But, finding all his propoſals rejected with diſdain, he reſolved to anticipate his enemy's deſigns, and carry the war into their dominions, rather than wait their attacking him in his own. The poſſeſſion of Saxony is not only convenient, but almoſt neceſſary, in order to invade Bohemia with ſucceſs. His majeſty therefore determined to occupy it; he was the more confirmed in this reſolution, as he knew the elector had tacitely concurred in all the ſchemes concerted for his ruin, and waited only for a ſure opportunity to concur alſo in the execution.

WITH this view, an army, conſiſting of near ſeventy battalions and eighty ſquadrons, divided into three different corps, entered the electorate on the 29th of Auguſt: the right wing compoſed one, and marched, under the command of prince Ferdinand of Brunſwic, from the duchy of Magdeburg, by Hall, Leipſig, Borna, Chemnitz, Friberg, and Dippoldiſwalda, and thence towards Dreſden, the place deſigned for the rendezvous of the army. The center, commanded

commanded by the king in person, composed the second corps, and marched on the left of the Elbe, by Wittenberg, Torgau, Meissen, and thence by Kesselsdorff to Dresden. The left wing formed the third corps, and was commanded by the duke of Bevern, who marched from the neighbourhood of Frankfort on the Oder, by Elsterwerda, Bautzen, Stolpen, and Lohmen, and there encamped on the right of the Elbe opposite to Pirna. The whole Prussian army assembled in the neighbourhood of Dresden, on the 6th of September. His majesty's intention seems to have been to persuade the king of Poland to join him in attacking Bohemia, or, which is more probable, in case of a refusal, to have a pretence for seizing Saxony, as it really happened soon after.

The disposition of the king's march into Saxony, we think very fine, as there was not above 15,000 men in that country; which were not assembled, as yet, in a body; and, even had they been so, they were still inferior to either of the king's columns, nor could they advance against any one of them without being cut off from Dresden by the other two, as appears evident from the inspection of the map of that country.

The event confirmed the goodness of the disposition; the Saxons were obliged to abandon the whole country; and at last they united, to the number of about 14,000 men, in the well-known camp of Pirna. His Polish majesty had chosen this position because it was thought impregnable; and, as he imagined, secured a communication with Bohemia; from whence only he could expect any succours, and where he could retire in case of necessity.

Encouraged by these considerations, he resolved to reject the proposals made him by the king of Prussia; how honestly we will not pretend to determine, but not wisely, as will evidently appear when we come to give our observations on this transaction.

The king of Pruſſia, who propoſed invading Bohemia, and reducing it to his obedience before the empreſs could aſſemble her troops, or any of the other confederates be in a condition to attack him, had, on his entering Saxony, ordered marſhal Schwerin, at the head of an army, conſiſting of thirty-three battalions and fifty-five ſquadrons, to enter that province by the way of Nachod and Neuſtadt. But, finding the Saxons would not come into his terms, and were ſo advantageouſly encamped that he could not force them, he found it neceſſary to change his plan of operations.

He did not think it ſafe to penetrate into Bohemia and leave the Saxons maſters of the Elbe behind him, as he had no magazines in that country; nor could he convey, what little was to be found, over thoſe immenſe defiles into Bohemia, not having tranſports ſufficient for that purpoſe. For theſe reaſons he reſolved to reduce the Saxons before he advanced any further; to prevent them from receiving any ſuccours; ſecure a paſſage for himſelf, when found neceſſary; and obſerve the motions of the Auſtrians. A conſiderable corps, firſt under the command of prince Ferdinand of Brunſwic, and afterwards under that of marſhal Keith, was ſent to take poſt at Johnſdorff in Bohemia. Marſhal Schwerin was ordered to keep his poſition at Aujeſt, oppoſite to Königſgratz. This, the king juſtly imagined, would oblige the Auſtrians to ſend an army on that ſide to oppoſe his further progreſs; and, if they thus divided their forces, their efforts to diſengage the Saxons, ſhould they attempt it, as moſt probably they would, muſt be much leſs formidable.

The empreſs, either with an intention to conceal her deſigns againſt the king of Pruſſia 'till ſhe and her allies were ſufficiently prepared to execute them, or from the uncertain, ſlow, and dilatory counſels of her miniſtry, had not as yet aſſembled any conſiderable forces in Bohemia: however, on the motions of the Pruſſians, ſhe

she ordered all those that were then in the country to form two camps: the smallest, commanded by prince Piccolomini, at Königsgratz, to oppose Schwerin: the greatest, commanded by marshal Brown, at Kollin, which was destined to march as soon as possible to the relief of the Saxons.

The king encamped at Grofs Zedlitz, in the neighbourhood of Pirna: his whole care was to block up the Saxons, and reduce them by famine, as he could not attack them with any probability of success. In this he succeeded to his wish; for, before the end of September, they were reduced to the most deplorable condition, and in want of every thing.

The empress, informed of their situation, and knowing that it depended on that army, whether Bohemia or Saxony should be made the seat of war, ordered M. Brown to march, and attempt to relieve them at any rate. Upon this the marshal quitted his camp at Kollin, and arrived the 23d of September at Budyn on the Egra, in order to be at hand to concert measures with the Saxons for succouring them. Here he was forced to remain 'till the 30th, to wait for the artillery and pontoons, then preparing at Vienna.

In this situation things continued 'till the 28th, when his majesty, accompanied by some general officers, went to marshal Keith's camp, in order to examine that position, and change it, if any motions of the enemy should make it necessary, and then return to the camp at Pirna. But, while he was here, advice was brought him, that M. Brown, having at length got his artillery and pontoons, was preparing to pass the Egra; which shewed plainly his intention of relieving the Saxons.

The king thought he could not frustrate this design more effectually, than by advancing further into Bohemia, and force M. Brown back, by a battle, if necessary. His majesty, therefore, ordered his vanguard, consisting of eleven squadrons, 400 hussars, and

and six battalions, to march on the 29th of September from the camp of Johnsdorff, and occupy that at Tirmitz, beyond the ravin and river at Aussig. Being here further informed, that the enemy was to pass the Egra that very day, and encamp at Lowositz, he thought it necessary to pass the mountains of Bascopol and Kletchen, put the defiles behind him, and occupy the avenues leading into the plain before M. Brown's camp; that he might, without difficulty, advance and attack him, if he found it convenient; and therefore, as soon as the head of the army, which had been ordered to follow to Tirmitz, appeared, he, on the 30th in the morning, with the vanguard, set out for Welmina; where the whole army arrived, without any other difficulty but the badness of the roads, at eight o'clock at night.

The king fearing the enemy would march in the night, and occupy the mountains of Radostitz and Lobosch, and, by taking such a position, not only make it impossible to attack them, but force his majesty to fall back to Aussig, which could not be done without the utmost difficulty, he resumed his march, passed the ravin, and occupied the mountains on the other side; the vanguard in C. C. and the rest of the army in G. G. where they remained the whole night, in the order they had marched; it being too late to camp, and the more so as the ground had not been sufficiently reconnoitred.

The first of October, in the morning, the Prussian army, consisting of sixty-five squadrons, twenty-six battalions, and 102 pieces of cannon, was formed in I. I. the infantry in two lines, and the cavalry in three, behind; as well for want of ground, as from its nature, which rendered it improper for cavalry to act in.

The right wing of the infantry was posted in the village of Radostitz, at the foot of a hill of the same name. Before this is another hill, called the Homolkaberg, which, though much lower than

than the former, is however so high that it commands all the plain underneath, as far as the village of Sulowitz. The king afterwards advanced his right wing to this hill, and placed a battery of heavy cannon upon it.

The center occupied the valley formed by that mountain and the Loboschberg, on which the left wing was posted: this last mountain is prodigiously high and steep, and runs into the plain, almost to Lowositz. The side of it is covered with vineyards, which are separated by stone walls; in these M. Brown had posted some thousand Croats, who were sustained by several battalions of Hungarian infantry; K. K. parallel to these mountains, and at some few hundred yards distant from the foot of them, runs a marshy rivulet, which in many places spreads itself in the plain, and forms several large lakes; between this rivulet and the hills, on which the Prussian army was formed, runs also a very deep ravin, from Sulowitz to Lowositz. The only passes over this rivulet and ravin are at these two villages, and over a narrow stone bridge between them. The ground behind this rivulet rises a little, particularly towards Sulowitz; on this the Austrian army B. B. consisting of seventy-two squadrons, fifty-two battalions, and ninety-eight pieces of cannon, was posted. It was formed in two lines, and a corps de reserve: the infantry was in the center, and the cavalry on the wings, as usual; that on the right, however, a little before the action began, marched forwards, and occupied the plain N. N. on the left of the village of Lowositz, L. L. M. Brown had ordered this village to be fortified, and had placed some of his best infantry in it, with a prodigious quantity of artillery. He had likewise raised a large battery, and some redoubts, on the plain before it. By this means he thought he had rendered his right inattackable; his center, and left, covered by the marshy rivulet, and the ravin above-mentioned, were

in

in reality so; and therefore he resolved to wait the event in that position.

As to the king's disposition we have nothing to say; excepting that from the beginning he ought to have placed his cavalry in the center, from Lobofchberg to Kinitz; this would have enabled him to leave more infantry upon the Homolka mountain, and to have reinforced still more his left, where he proposed making his chief effort. From this position he might have sustained those squadrons he sent to attack the enemy's horse, whereas they could be of no use behind the infantry, as they could not, in that situation, protect it, in case they were repulsed at Lowofitz.

The king's activity in marching from Johnsdorff to Welmina shews he knew how important it was to put the defile behind him; a general maxim, when you advance towards an enemy, which we presume to recommend, for reasons too obvious, in our opinion, to require an explanation.

The Austrians should, we think, have sent some heavy artillery on the right of the Elbe, and have placed a battery, as we have represented in the plan; this would have taken the Prussian infantry in flank, while they advanced through the plain, from the Lobofchberg, to attack Lowofitz. Why the Austrian horse passed the ravin to attack the Prussians in Q. Q. we cannot conceive; as it could not serve any purpose whatever.

The action begun, about seven in the morning, between the Prussian's left wing, and the troops which M. Brown had posted in the Lobofchberg; and was sustained by an irregular fire, without any considerable advantage on either side 'till near 12 o'clock: then the day, which had been so foggy that nothing could be distinguished at the distance of a hundred yards, began to clear up. A large body of Austrian horse N. N. was discovered in the plain by Lowofitz, as well as some infantry in and about that village,

and

and at the redoubts and battery. As no regular line appeared then, the king thought it was only the rear-guard; and he was the more perſuaded of this, becauſe, from ſome motions heard the night before, in the enemy's camp, he imagined the army had either paſſed the Elbe at Leutmeritz, or was retired back to the old camp at Budyn. To be certain, however, he ordered a regiment of dragoons and ſome horſe O. O. to paſs through the intervals of the infantry and attack that cavalry. They did ſo in Q. Q. and drove them back beyond the ravin: in purſuing them, they advanced ſo far, that they were expoſed to a heavy cannonade from Lowoſitz and Sulowitz, and it was with great difficulty and loſs that they could retire under the protection of their infantry in R. from whence they were commanded to reſume their firſt poſition behind the line.

By this time the fog was intirely diſſipated, and the Auſtrian army appeared very clearly, in the poſition we have ſhewn in the annexed plan.

The king, having examined it for ſome time, judged the right to be the weakeſt for many reaſons, and chiefly, by its being commanded from the Loboſchberg. He therefore ordered his ſecond line to enter into the firſt, with the cavalry in the center, that he might extend his front and occupy the Homolka and Loboſchberg in force: this being ſoon executed, the whole army marched, inclining always to the left; from whence he propoſed making his attack. This left being reinforced, and protected by the fire of a very numerous and well-ſerved artillery, advanced down the Loboſchberg towards Lowoſitz, and with great eaſe drove the Croats K. K. though ſupported by the beſt of the Auſtrian infantry, out of the vineyards into the plain: this will appear very natural from the deſcription we have given of this mountain, which overlooked the vineyards in ſuch a manner, that the troops placed in them

could

could not raise their heads high enough to direct their shot at the Prussians while they came down, and consequently made but a feeble resistance.

M. Brown sent several battalions of his best infantry from his right to sustain them in the mountains; and general Lacy, who commanded them, made several vigorous, but fruitless, attacks at the foot of the mountain, in one of which he was wounded. At last he was convinced it was needless to renew the attempt, and therefore fell back towards Lowositz.

The Prussians, being now quite masters of the Lobofchberg, were ordered to halt at the foot of it, in order to reform the line, which had been a little disordered, as well by the action itself, as by the irregularity and difficulty of the ground, and to bring up the artillery: a precaution so necessary, that the neglect of it has very often been the cause of the loss of many battles which might have been won.

As soon as they were formed, they advanced in several lines S. S. towards Lowositz, keeping their left close to the Elbe to avoid the fire of the battery L. L. the right still continued on the Homolka mountain : by this disposition the enemy's left and center were prevented from attempting any thing on that side, and the king was enabled to withdraw his left without danger, if it was repulsed at Lowositz : which indeed was not very probable; because, from the situation of the ground, he could reinforce it with greater facility, and in much less time, than the enemy could his right: consequently could bring a greater number of men into action, at the same time, which generally must decide the fate of it.

Marshal Brown, believing that the victory depended on his being able to keep Lowositz, threw almost his whole right wing into it, and about it; the action therefore was here, long and obstinate; at length however it was determined in favour of the

Prussians,

Pruffians, and chiefly by the help of their artillery, which had fet the village on fire. This circumftance, and the want of ground to form upon, put the Auftrians in confufion; and, as they could not be fuftained by a proper line for want of room, the communications not having been made broad enough to permit three or four battalions to march up in front to fupport them, they were forced to abandon it, and fall back with precipitation on their cavalry.*

MARSHAL Brown, feeing his right wing forced, ordered his left to advance through the village of Sulowitz W. W. and attack the enemy's right: this they attempted to execute, but in vain; a fmall number only of the infantry could pafs the village; and thofe were unable to form on the other fide under the fire of a numerous heavy artillery, which played on them from the battery on the Homolka mountain, within a few hundred yards of the damm over which they were to pafs the marfhy rivulet at Sulowitz: the few who had paffed were therefore obliged to fall back inftantly into the village, which they repaffed in confufion, as many houfes were already on fire.

THIS attempt of the marfhal's was too unreafonable to have been undertaken with any other view, as we think, than merely to draw the enemy's attention that way, and gain time to put his right in fome order, and facilitate a retreat.

THIS he executed in a mafterly manner, V. V. He ordered his center and left to make a movement to the right, by which they occupied the ground, in the inftant the right quitted it, behind Lowofitz.

---

* When a village is intended to be fupported, the retrenchment muft be feparated from the houfes by an interval, fufficient for the troops to form in, between the houfes and retrenchments; and the village muft be cleared behind, that you may march two or more battalions in front, otherwife you cannot defend it; the inftant 'tis put on fire you muft abandon it in fuch confufion as fometimes communicates to the whole line.

Lowofitz. This infantry, fuftained by the right wing of the cavalry, covered the retreat fo effectually, that no attempt was made to trouble it.

THE marfhal took a new pofition a little further back: the left and center continued at fome diftance behind the marfhy rivulets, and the right formed an angle with the line, having the front towards the plain, behind Lowofitz and the Elbe. So that the enemy could not pafs through Lowofitz and form on the plain, with his rear immediately on the Elbe, under the fire of a numerous artillery; and the lefs fo, as, to form fuch a line, his battalions and fquadrons muft have prefented their flank in marching to take up their ground.

THESE reafons induced, or rather forced, the king to remain fatisfied with the advantage he had gained, and keep his line behind Lowofitz, X. X. While marfhal Brown continued in this pofition, the king had by no means effected his defign. The action was not any ways decifive, and therefore had not made it impoffible for M. Brown to attempt the relief of the Saxons. He was now juft as much in a condition to undertake it as before the action, his lofs having been inferior to that of the Pruffians; neither could the king attack him with any probability of fuccefs, as he muft, in paffing the marfhy rivulet, expofe his army to thofe difficulties which M. Brown had, by experience, found unfurmountable.

FROM this very embarraffing fituation his majefty's fuperior talents extricated him. He fent the duke of Bevern with a large body of horfe and foot to Tfchifkovitz, as if he propofed turning the enemy's left flank, and hemm them in between the Elbe and the Egra. This manœuvre had its defired effect. Marfhal Brown, fearing the event, haftened to repafs this laft river, and occupy his old camp at Budyn, which he did without any lofs.

Thus ended the battle of Lowofitz, which begun at 7 o'clock, and ended at three. Both parties claim the victory. It muſt however be confeſſed that the Pruſſians have the beſt right to it, if we judge from the conſequences of the action, which is the only certain rule to go by in ſimilar caſes.

The Auſtrians did certainly intend to diſengage the Saxons, and with that view advanced to Lowofitz. The king could have no other object in view than to prevent their executing this plan. This end was obtained by the battle of Lowofitz, and the ſubſequent manœuvres, which forced the Auſtrians back behind the Egra, and ſo hindered them from undertaking any thing of conſequence for the relief of their friends the Saxons. Had the Pruſſians gained a more compleat victory, they would have been enabled to take their winter quarters in Bohemia.

The loſs of the Auſtrians on this occaſion amounted to 19 officers, 420 private men, killed: 105 officers, 1729 men, wounded: 711 miſſing, or taken priſoners: and 475 horſes killed and wounded: in all, 2984. Among the dead was count Radicati,* lieutenant general of horſe, who commanded the right wing. Among the wounded and miſſing was major general prince Lobowitz, and many field officers. Among the many who diſtinguiſhed themſelves, Marſhal Brown, in his letter to the empreſs, takes particular notice of general Odonell,† who, after the death of Radicati, commanded the right wing of the cavalry, prince Löwenſtein, Lacy, &c. &c. The loſs of the Pruſſians, in the cavalry, amounted

to

---

* Count Radicati was born in Piemont. In 1739 he was lieutenant colonel in Vernes's horſe; wounded at the battle of Grotzka; in 1740 was made a colonel; in 1745 a major general; in 1751 he obtained a regiment; and in 1754 a lieutenant general. He had the reputation of a good officer, and particularly for his talents in exerciſing the troops.

† Count Odonell is born of a very good family in Ireland: he was for ſome time lieutenant colonel in Ollone's dragoons; in 1742 a colonel of Baleyra's; in 1746 a major general, as a recompence for his bravery and conduct at the battle of Parma. In the expedition

againſt

in GERMANY, 1756.   13

to 11 officers, 281 private men, killed: 28 officers, 424 men, wounded: 8 officers, 238 private men, prisoners. In the infantry, 5 officers, 423 men, killed: 53 officers, 1374 men, wounded: 5 officers, 458 men, taken prisoners. In all, 3308. Among the dead were major generals Oertzen,* Lúderitz,† and Quadt.‡ And among the wounded was lieutenant general Kleist, ‖ who died soon after of his wounds.

MARSHAL Brown, having failed in his attempt to relieve the Saxons on the left of the Elbe, resolved to try his fortune on the right.

---

against Provence he commanded a detached corps with reputation. In this battle he commanded the right wing during the greatest part of the action, and distinguished himself very much, for which he had a regiment given him, and was made a lieutenant general. We shall have occasion to mention this gentleman often, in the course of this work, with great applause.

* This gentleman was major general of horse: he had in his youth studied at Halle, in Saxony: he was a long time a standard bearer and subalter in the gens d'armes; in 1725 a captain of horse; in 1739 a major; in 1741 a lieutenant colonel: and having distinguished himself at the battle of Soor he had the ordre pour le merite; in 1745 was a colonel; in 1750 a major general; in 1752 had a regiment given him: at this battle he received three wounds in the head, of which he died the next day.

† Major general Lúderitz was born in 1699. In 1715 was an under officer in the Potsdam guard; in 1719 a cornet; in 1725 a captain of horse; in 1740 a major; in 1743 a lieutenant colonel, and distinguished himself very much at the battles of Hohenfriedberg and Kesselsdorff; in 1745 a colonel; in 1752 a major general. His body was tore to pieces by a cannon ball.

‡ Baron Quadt was in 1728 a major; in 1736 a lieutenant colonel; in 1743 a colonel; in 1747 a major general; and then obtained a regiment.

‖ Lieutenant general Kleist was born in 1688. In 1702 he was a cadet; in 1708 wounded in the foot, which left the bone crooked for ever after; soon after he went into the Palatin service, and served the war in Flanders 'till the peace in 1712; in 1716 he returned into the Prussian service; in 1724 was made a major; in 1729 he went as volunteer to Corsica; in 1738 was lieutenant colonel; in 1742 a colonel, and was in almost all the actions of that war in Silesia; in 1745 a major general; in 1747 had a regiment; in 1756 a lieutenant general. In the battle of Lowositz he was wounded; he continued however on horseback, without binding his wounds, 'till 4 o'clock. Soon after the king gave him the order of the black eagle. He died of his wounds in January following at Dresden.

right. It was agreed that the Saxons should pass the Elbe, the 11th of October in the night, near Königstein; and that the marshal should attack the Prussians at Ratmansdorff and Borsdorff the 12th in the morning, while the Saxons did the same on their side. Accordingly he, at the head of about 8000 men, passed the Elbe near Raudnitz, and marched by Neustadtel, Romburg, and Hanspach, and arrived at Lichtenhayn, where he encamped, waiting to hear the Prussians and Saxons engaged, (which he knew must happen the instant these last passed the Elbe) that he might likewise enter into action, and execute his part of the concerted plan.

The weather had been so remarkably rainy and stormy, that the Saxons could not effect their passage over the Elbe 'till the 13th at four o'clock in the morning, and then with much difficulty and loss of time. This gave the Prussians an opportunity of reinforcing all their posts on the right of the Elbe, so that the Saxons found themselves opposed by forces much superior to what they expected. The ground on the right side of the Elbe, about Pirna and Königstein, is intersected by high mountains, covered with thick woods; they are separated by deep ravins, formed by the rain in autumn, and by the melting snow in the beginning of summer; there are consequently very few practicable roads. These the Prussians had occupied, and fortified, with the utmost care, by retrenchments, abattis, &c.

Among these great mountains is the Lilienstein, extremely high, and so near the Elbe, that there is no room to form upon between the foot of it and the banks of the river; and only one very narrow road.

The Saxons passed the Elbe opposite to this mountain, and endeavoured to form; but the want of room did not permit it; and therefore they lay together in confusion, on and about a small eminence, near the village of Ebenheit. From this situation, surrounded

rounded by every difficulty which art and nature could oppose, it was justly, as we think, judged impossible for them to extricate themselves.

The Prussians, in the mean time, had entered the camp of Pirna early in the morning of the 13th, where they found the rear-guard of the Saxons, and most of the baggage; both fell into their hands, the bridge having been broke before any considerable part of them could pass: destitute of every resource, extenuated with hunger and cold, having been under arms from the 12th at night 'till the 14th in the morning, deprived of all hopes of being succoured by M. Brown, who now informed them of his being only at Lichtenhayn, and that he could not advance any nearer, it was resolved to capitulate; he, on his part, having waited above two days without receiving any intelligence from the Saxons, thought it necessary to provide for his own safety, and therefore retired. He lost no more than 200 men in his retreat, which was trifling, if we consider that he might have been cut off entirely, had the Prussians, encamped at Lowositz, been a little more vigilant; because they might have passed the Elbe, behind him, near Lowositz, or Leutmeritz.

During this transaction the king arrived, the 14th in the morning, at his army in Saxony, and, after much negotiating, a treaty was concluded with the king of Poland on the 18th, by which it was stipulated, that the Saxon army should disperse, and engage not to serve against the king of Prussia, who was to remain master of Saxony; and that the king of Poland should have leave to retire into that kingdom.

The king of Prussia having thus accomplished his designs, for this campaign, ordered his armies to quit Bohemia. This was accordingly done before the end of the month. That commanded by marshal Schwerin fell back into Silesia, and cantoned on the frontiers of Bohemia from Zuckmantel to Greiffenberg. That under the king cantoned in Saxony, and formed a chain from Egra to Pirna, and from thence through Lusace, as far as the Queiss.

Thus ended the campaign of 1756, which lasted only two months; the transactions of it however justly demand our attention, as well for the reputation of the generals, as for the importance of its event; we shall therefore give our observations on the one, and the other.

The king of Prussia seems to have committed some faults, both as a politician, and as a general. He had known, a long time before he entered Saxony, that a formidable confederacy was forming against him; and yet it does not appear that he ever attempted to make any alliance to counterballance it, and render its effect vain; which, considering the great ascendency he had acquired in Europe, he might probably have done.

He confided too much in himself, and had too despicable an opinion of his enemies, which might, and indeed ought, naturally to have proved fatal to him.

The next fault that occurs is, that he did not begin the war in 1755, or at least in April 1756; he was then as well prepared, as in the month of August, when he entered Saxony; whereas his enemies were infinitely less so.*

His negotiating with the king of Poland, before and after he entered Saxony, we believe, was intended only to amuse that prince, and prevent him from taking any measures that might obstruct or retard his operations against the Austrians, who no doubt were the
only

---

* We think it a general rule that you ought to begin the campaign as soon as possible; because, if you are on the offensive, you will have time to execute whatever you have proposed to do: if on the defensive, 'tis no less necessary to enter into the field as soon as possible; because, if you are beforehand with the enemy, you consume the forage, and destroy the country from whence he is to live. Add, that you gain time, and make him lose the campaign in driving you out of his country; and, when he has effected it, 'tis too late to undertake any thing against your's.

only object of his projects at this time. Our reasons for this opinion are, that, by the tenor and manner of this negotiation, there does not appear the least tendency to a composition, but on condition of his remaining master of Saxony, and of that army being dispersed, which no doubt he was resolved to accomplish, that he might proceed to invade Bohemia with greater hopes of success.

WHETHER we consider this transaction in a political, or a military light, it will appear to have been a prudent and wise measure. He knew too much of the sentiments of the Saxon court, with regard to himself, and of the part they took in the confederacy formed against him, to confide in any offers they made him. He could not prudently leave an army of 14,000 men behind him. For, though the king of Poland promised to disperse them, he could with ease assemble them, and augment them at pleasure; and soon be in a condition to make the Prussian monarch repent of his imprudence.

THE possession of Saxony, considered in a military light, is of so much consequence, that it is not possible to attack the empress, on that side of her dominions, with the least probability of success, without it. Being extremely rich and populous, an army of 40,000 men can be raised and maintained by this electorate. Magazines may **be formed** on the Elbe, from whence an army in Bohemia may be **abundantly** supplied; **and**, by its position, if you are master of Silesia, you surround Bohemia in such a manner, that you force the empress to separate her armies into **so** many divisions, that she cannot oppose your entering that country, any where, with success, as appears from the wars carried on there at different times: whereas, if you are not master of Saxony, you can enter Bohemia on the side of Silesia only. This enables the empress to unite, in some measure, her forces, which are effectually covered by Olmutz and Prague, when forced to fall back; from whence they cover Austria; and in this case the king of Prussia must always leave an army on the Lower Elbe, to cover his own dominions on that side, lest the elector of Saxony, by force or persuasion, should be induced to join the Austrians.

For these reasons we think the invasion of Saxony was a wise measure; how far it may be consistent with justice, those, who are better acquainted with the laws of nations than we are, must determine.

From what has been said, it seems that the king of Prussia committed a capital fault, in not having marched into Bohemia, the moment he saw the Saxons determined to defend their camp at Pirna, and reject the terms which he proposed; because he must certainly know that the Austrian army was not assembled in any considerable numbers; and that it wanted artillery and stores; that it was posted at such a distance as made it impossible for M. Brown to oppose his entering into Bohemia, or stop his progress when he should be there; and therefore would fall back on the Danube, if pushed, as well to cover the capital, as to secure his communication with the troops he expected from Flanders, Italy, and Hungary. His majesty therefore would have found Bohemia abandoned; and, during the winter, he might with ease have reduced Prague and Olmutz; both which places being then quite unprovided, and incapable of opposing any considerable resistance.

The conquest of these two places would have enabled his majesty to begin the next campaign in Moravia, at least; and perhaps on the Danube; with the siege or blockade of Vienna: from whence he might, without any risk, have sent a considerable corps on the frontiers of Hungary; and the army, destined to guard Saxony, into the empire, between the sources of the Main and the Upper Danube. The first would have hindered the empress from receiving any succours from those countries: and the last would effectually
prevent

prevent those princes, who were his enemies, from uniting against him; encourage those who favoured him; overawe the French in Alsace, and on the Main; and raise such contributions as would have recruited and maintained his armies. Had his majesty taken these steps, he would have cut off all communication with Flanders and Hungary; and even with the Tyrol, if the army, which I suppose in the empire, sent a strong corps to occupy Passau and its castle, at the confluent of the Inn and the Danube; one of the most important posts on that river; which cuts off all communication between Vienna and the empire, overawes Upper Austria, as well as the Tyrol. The few resources left her imperial majesty would have been soon exhausted.

MARSHAL Belleisle, on the death of Charles VI. formed a plan for dividing his dominions.

THE French and Bavarians were to march down the Danube, through Upper Austria, to Vienna. The Prussians and Saxons were to enter Bohemia, and, having reduced it, proceed to Vienna likewise.

IN the first campaign the French and Bavarians entered Upper Austria, which they laid under contribution to the gates of Vienna. The Prussians and Saxons conquered Bohemia; and nothing could have prevented the entire and compleat execution of M. Belleisle's plan, but the ignorance of some of the chiefs, the weakness of cardinal Fleury, and the divisions among the allies.

THE king of Prussia being master of all the places on the Elbe, by leaving a small corps to watch the camp of Pirna, he made it impossible for the Saxons to undertake any thing against him. Supposing they quitted their camp, they could not subsist in Saxony, having neither places nor magazines of any kind; being at the same time continually harrassed by the corps, which we suppose, left there to observe them: much less could they advance into Bohemia, in order to join the Austrians; because they would find themselves inclosed between the king's army, and the corps left in Saxony. In the end, therefore, they must have dispersed of themselves.

His forces at this time were numerous, and he might with ease have brought 110,000 men into the field; 20,000 of which were more than sufficient to block up effectually the Saxons in their camp at Pirna, as appeared from the fact itself; for there was no more under prince Maurice when they were forced to capitulate: The remaining 90,000 were certainly more than sufficient to drive the Austrians to the Danube.

As the army under M. Schwerin was far superior to that under prince Piccolomini, and better provided with artillery, we think he ought to have attacked him; and, if he thought the camp of Königsgratz too strong, he might leave him there, and march, on the right of the Elbe, towards Brandeiss, or even approach Prague. This manœuvre would infallibly force M. Brown to quit his position on the Egra, and fall back to cover that place. M. Schwerin risk'd nothing by this motion, because Piccolomini was too weak to execute any solid enterprize in Silesia: and, as to subsistance, the marshal could never be in want; the country, being very fruitful, would have furnished him abundantly. Had what we here propose been executed, the Austrians must have abandoned the circles of Saatz, Leütmeritz, Buntzlau, and Königsgratz, in order to assemble their forces about Prague, and keep open their communication with the Danube; and, if we consider the very bad state of that army, it is probable they would have been forced back as far as Moravia: so that the king, even without coming to an action, would have been master of the greatest part of Bohemia, and have taken his winter quarters in that kingdom. Besides, the

Saxons,

Saxons, on seeing their friends forced back, would not have presumed to make any stand in the camp of Pirna.

As to the Auftrians, they seem to have committed many faults, and these such capital ones, as might have decided the fate of their empire, had the king of Pruffia taken the measures already indicated.

It was well known, even in the month of June, that the king intended attacking the Auftrian dominions. From the motions then made in the duchy of Magdeburg and the adjoining country, it was more than probable that part of his troops would march through Saxony. This should have determined the Auftrians to send an army there, in order to sustain the Saxons in that country, or at least facilitate their retreat into Bohemia. This being neglected, they should have occupied the defiles as far as the ravin of Ghifhubel, and those by Altenberg, by which a communication with the Saxons was kept open. Half the troops then in Bohemia, posted properly in those mountains, would have made it impossible for the Prussians either to reduce the Saxons, or to penetrate into Bohemia.

The rest of the army, destined to act on this side, should have encamped any where between the Egra and the abovementioned defiles, and have thrown bridges over the Elbe, in order to send their light troops, on the right of that river, as far as Schandau and Hohenstein.

This would have forced the king to fall back to Dresden. The next campaign the same difficulty would have occurred; and therefore, at last, he must have renounced to the hopes of entering Bohemia on that side; left an army to guard Saxony; and limit his operations to the side of Silesia only. By thus securing the mountains with 20,000 Auftrians, and the 14,000 Saxons, they could always enter Saxony, and probably re-occupy it, considering that the army of the empire could assemble on the Saala, and with ease penetrate into that country by Voightland, on the Prussians right flank; who, not being covered by any fortress on that side, must fall back towards Wittemberg, and perhaps farther down. This furnished an opportunity of retaking all the places on the Elbe; and of sending a corps, through Lusace, into the marquisate of Brandeburg. The position of Groffenhayn cuts off all communication between Silesia and Saxony, and rendered that between Silesia and Brandeburg precarious; because the light troops, sustained by the army at Groffenhayn, could have made incursions as far as the Oder. Piccolomini's corps, if properly posted, was strong enough to oppose Schwerin, and prevent his undertaking any thing of consequence; which probably he had no intention to do, while the king was hindered from entering Bohemia.

Having neglected to occupy the defiles leading to Pirna, it became impossible to relieve the Saxons, at least on the left of the Elbe; because twelve or fifteen battalions, which the king posted any where between Lowositz and Pirna, could not be forced by an attack on their front; and, if you attempted to turn their right wing, by sending a corps over the mountains at Altenberg, it is so far off that the enemy might, either from his troops in Bohemia, or from those in Saxony, anticipate you. We cannot, therefore, conceive why marshal Brown did not occupy some of these defiles, as, in our opinion, the success of this campaign, and perhaps of the war, depended on this step.

Since these precautions were not taken, it was certainly in vain to attempt any thing on that side of the Elbe. The only thing remaining to be done, in our opinion, was to have left 20,000 men in the camp at Budyn; with a corps, composed chiefly of light troops, to push into the mountains beyond Lowositz, and into those of Altenberg, to draw the Prussians attention that way;

and

and with the remainder pafs on the right, (leaving fomething to mafk the bridge at Leutmeritz, and obferve the enemy in the mountains, between Lowofitz and Auffig) and march on that fide to Schandau and Hohenftein, and attack the Pruffians pofted at Ratmanfdorff, and on the Lilienftein.

These pofts were very weak on that fide, and fortified only towards the Elbe, to oppofe the Saxons, and therefore could not have refifted one inftant; efpecially if, at the fame time, the Saxons made any confiderable effort. By this manœuvre the communication would have been eafily opened; and the Pruffians on that fide, if purfued with vigour, could not have retired without lofs, having no more than one bridge, at Pirna, by which they could be fuccoured; on which a falfe attack might have been made through the foreft of Löhmen, as well to prevent fuccours, as to alarm the Pruffians; this probably would have made them abandon their other pofts, for fear of lofing their communication with the army encamped on the other fide of the Elbe.

The junction with the Saxons being once effected, and all the right of the Elbe, as far as Pirna, occupied by the Auftrians, his majefty muft have fallen back inftantly into Saxony, or have perifhed in the mountains with cold and hunger.

Marshal Brown rifqued nothing by this manœuvre, as the king, with the fmall army he had then in Bohemia, would not have prefumed to pafs the Egra and attack the 20,000 men left there; becaufe, by fuch an attempt, he would give the Auftrian general an opportunity of repaffing the Elbe, and occupy the defiles behind him, relieve the Saxons, and probably reduce his majefty to the melancholy neceffity of feeing his own army and that of prince Maurice, thus feparated, beat in detail.

He attempted, as we have faid, to relieve the Saxons with 8000 men only, and could not fucceed.

We

WE now come to examine the battle itself, wherein the conduct of M. Brown does not seem, by any means, equal to the reputation he had acquired.

FROM the description we have given of the ground, it appears evident, that the marshal could not possibly obtain any other advantage, than perhaps to repulse the enemy; which, from the bad choice of his camp, was very improbable. But, even supposing he had beat him back as far as the vineyards on the Lobofchberg, -he certainly could never have forced him from thence, and from the Homolka mountain; because, to form these two attacks, he must have filed through the villages of Lowofitz and Sulowitz, and have formed between those villages and the mountains upon which the Prussian army, with above 100 pieces of cannon, was posted, and in many places within musket-shot of the ground where the Austrians must have formed. I appeal therefore to all military gentlemen, whether in these circumstances such a manœuvre was possible.

ADD to this, that the king, though repulsed, could without any danger have sent a strong corps on M. Brown's left, which would have rendered his communication with the Egra so precarious, that he must have fallen back behind that river, as it really happened the night after the action; for it was the sending the duke of Bevern with a corps to Tschiskovitz, rather than any advantage gained in the battle, which forced M. Brown to repass the Egra. From whence it appears, that, though the Austrians repulsed the king, it contributed nothing at all to the relief of the Saxons; because they could not detach, from that or any other camp between the mountains and the Egra, 20,000 men, and less would not do without exposing the remainder to certain ruin.

HAVING

HAVING neglected to occupy the mountains of Lobofch and Homolka, which he might have done, many hours, before the enemy appeared, the only thing remaining to be done, was to have paffed the Elbe, the night before the battle, with the whole army, leaving fome light troops to amufe the king; thefe, on being pufhed, retired to Budyn.

IN this cafe M. Brown might have detached fuch a corps to Schandau, as would certainly have opened a communication with the Saxons, and probably have deftroyed all the Pruffians on that fide of the Elbe: with the remainder he covered the whole country effectually, excepting thofe few villages between the mountains and the Egra, which the king would not have dared to pafs, becaufe, having no magazines in the country, and fubfifting only, at leaft chiefly, from what came from Saxony, he could not advance, with an army of about 25,000 men, into an enemy's country, leaving one fuperior mafter of the defiles, between him and his other army, fubfiftance, ftores, &c. without expofing himfelf to certain ruin.

THE pofition, therefore, taken at Lowofitz, was, in our opinion, as bad as poffible; nothing could be more inconfiftent, with the general theory of war, than to occupy a camp commanded by any neighbouring hills, and where it was impoffible to bring as many men into action, at the fame time, and in the fame point, as the enemy; who, on the contrary, had ground enough to form two thirds of his army to attack Lowofitz; whereas the Auftrians could bring a very few battalions, only, to fuftain it.

THE left and center were inattackable; the only point to be fuftained was Lowofitz. This the marfhal faw; but did not fee that it could not be defended, becaufe it was commanded by the Lobofchberg.

If the enemy was repulsed, you could not pursue him, either with cavalry or infantry.

If we consider this position, relative to the relief of the Saxons, the only object then in view, none could be less proper; because, by no one manœuvre possible, could M. Brown relieve them, though he had repulsed the enemy, who might have taken fifty camps between that place and the Saxons, from whence they would have hindered all communication between them and the Austrians.

We shall therefore conclude, that, in the choice of this camp, M. Brown acted inconsistent with the general rules of war; and with the particular ones, which the nature of the country, and the object he had in view, prescribed.

We hope our readers will not accuse us of presumption, for having, thus freely, given our opinion of the actions of those men, whose reputation is so well established. What we have said is certainly founded upon facts, and consistent with the nature of the country; and, as we think, with the principles of war: we therefore submit our reflections to those who are acquainted with the one and the other. For this purpose, we have furnished them with an exact plan and description of the ground where the battle was fought.

This, with their own knowledge of the military art, will enable them to decide how far our history of this campaign, and our remarks upon its various operations, are reasonable, or otherwise.

Great preparations were made, on both sides, for the ensuing campaign: the empress ordered the troops that lay in Hungary, Italy, and Flanders, to march into Bohemia: all the regiments of hussars were augmented to 1500 men; and those of the cavalry to 1000: two of the former, and one of Hungarian infantry, were new raised: to these were joined, two regiments of infantry, sent

by

by the elector of Magence and the Bishop of Wurtzburg, several pulks* of Uhlans,† and three regiments of Saxon light horse: all which, with what was already in Bohemia, formed an immense army, which, according to many gazettes, amounted to above 180,000 men, and was to be commanded by prince Charles of Lorrain.

THE Prussians, on their side, were no less diligent and active. The king found it absolutely necessary to get some light troops, to oppose those of his enemies, which were extremely numerous, and had given him much trouble, both in this and the preceding war; and therefore orders were given to raise four battalions of light infantry, which were augmented very much during the course of the war.

THERE happened in the winter some considerable actions between the light troops; which, though conducted with much valour and prudence on both sides, do not deserve any particular detail; because, in general, they have little or no influence on the success of a war, however necessary in an army: and, though they do not contribute essentially to the good or bad issue of a campaign, there is no doing without them. We shall therefore proceed to give an account of the operations of the campaign of 1757.

---

* A pulk amounts to about 800 men.

† Uhlans are inhabitants of the Uckraine, and chiefly Mahometans. In person, dress, and manner of fighting, they resemble the Tartars, Calmucks, &c. They are armed with pistols, sabres, a lance 15 foot long, and sometimes with a bow and arrow, instead of a carabine.

CAMPAIGN of 1757.

THE confederacy, formed against the king of Prussia, was now augmented, by the accession of Sweden and the Germanic body; whose united forces amounted to 700,000 men; whereas those of his majesty, and his allies, did not exceed 260,000.

As many of his enemies could not begin their operations until the season was far advanced, his majesty resolved to take the field as soon as possible; that he might, with his united forces, attack the nearest, and indeed the most considerable of them; the empress of Germany. If he had the good fortune to strike some blow of consequence in the beginning of the campaign, it was very probable this would retard, at least, and perhaps put an intire stop to, the operations of the other confederates.

These motives, which made it necessary for his Prussian majesty to bring matters immediately to a conclusion, made it equally so for the empress to embrace a contrary system.

She therefore determined to remain on the defensive, until her allies took the field, which she knew would oblige the king to divide his forces into so many parts, as would make it impossible for him to oppose, any where, a considerable resistance. This favourable circumstance she proposed waiting for, in order to begin her operations. In the mean time, nothing more was intended, than to provide for the defence of her dominions.

With this view M. Brown distributed the army into four different corps: the first, commanded by the duke of Aremberg, was posted at Egra; the second, under the marshal himself, at Budyn; the third, under count Königseg, at Reichenberg; and the fourth, under count Serbelloni, in Moravia.

By this disposition the marshal thought he could effectually cover Bohemia; as each of these corps was very considerable, and might with ease be assembled in some central position, to stop the progress of the enemy, should he attempt to advance; which it seems the marshal did not expect he would or could do; otherwise, we think, he never would have permitted his magazines to be formed almost on the frontiers, against the most common rules of military prudence.

His majesty, having resolved to penetrate into Bohemia, ordered his army to assemble in four different corps likewise: the one, under prince Maurice, at Chemnitz; the other, under himself, at Lockwitz; the third, under the prince of Bevern, at Zittau; and the fourth, under marshal Schwerin, in Silesia.

As these corps were very strong, his majesty thought he might with safety order them to enter Bohemia separately; but, for fear of exposing them to be beat in detail, the two first were to unite, the moment they passed the defiles, between the mountains about Lowositz and the Egra; and the two last were to do the same on the Iser, about Turnau: then it was thought, that the four corps, thus united into two, might proceed, without any risk, towards Prague; where the whole was to join.

The king, fearing that the enemy should send a body of infantry to occupy the defiles in the mountains, between Lockwitz and Lowositz, which might make it difficult, and perhaps impossible, for him to pass them, ordered prince Maurice to penetrate into the circle of Saatz, and instantly occupy them on the side of Bohemia, which would necessarily force the enemy to abandon them, for fear of being hemmed in between the two corps.

Things being thus concerted, prince Maurice quitted his station at Chemnitz, in the beginning of April, and marched by Zwickau and Plauen towards Egra; as if he intended attacking that place, or at least penetrate that way into Bohemia. To confirm the duke of Aremberg in this opinion, he ordered his light troops to engage some considerable action at Wildstein, the duke's quarters. Upon which this general threw himself into Egra, and ordered his corps to assemble in that neighbourhood. In the mean time prince Maurice returned in haste back to Auerbach; where, for greater celerity, he divided his corps into two columns; the one of which marched by Eibenstock Schwarzenberg to Gottesgabe, and from thence over the Kupferberg to Commottau; the other went over the Schneeberg Schlettau, Annaberg, and Basberg, likewise to Commottau; from whence he marched by Brix and Bilin to Linay, where he joined the king, on the 23d of April, who had likewise passed the mountains without meeting any considerable obstacle : the few Austrians who were posted at Aussig, under general Draskovitz, having been forced to quit that place on the approach of the king's army.

As the camp of Budyn is very strong, being covered by the Egra, his majesty did not think it adviseable to attempt any thing against it in front; he therefore marched higher up the river, towards Koschtitz, where bridges were thrown over it, and on the 26th in the morning the whole army passed.

HERE the light troops, and vanguard, met those of the duke of Aremberg, who was then coming from Egra, and proposed either encamping there, or go and join M. Brown at Budyn; but, on meeting the king here, he fell back towards Welwarn.

M. BROWN, finding the king had passed the Egra, and was encamped on his left flank, thought it necessary to quit his position at Budyn and retire to Prague, which was executed without any loss.

Upon which the king ordered the bridge at Budyn to be repaired, that he might with greater eafe receive his convoys; and then directed his fteps likewife to Prague, where he arrived the 2d of May, and took his camp on the Weiffenberg, on the left of the Moldau, which the Auftrians, now commanded by prince Charles, had quitted, and paffed on the other fide of the river.

While thefe things were paffing on the fide of Saxony, the prince of Bevern put his corps in motion on the 20th of April, and marched the fame day from Zittau to Reichenberg, where he found count Königfeg, with a body of near 20,000 men, encamped in a valley formed by two very high mountains; the breadth of it, in this place, does not exceed three Englifh miles; through the middle of it runs the river Neifs; into which many rivulets, or rather torrents, coming from the mountains, fall. Thefe mountains are covered with thick woods, which make it very difficult for any kind of troops to pafs them; for which reafons the Auftrian general occupied the valley from one fide to the other, having each wing extended only to the foot of the mountains: the right was on a rifing ground, which was fortified with fome redoubts, and covered by a deep ravin on the right of the Neifs: the center was on the left of the river, and alfo covered by a deep ravin, and fome redoubts: between the left of this ravin and the foot of the mountain, on that fide, is a fmall plain; here the cavalry was pofted in three lines, there not being room to extend them. On the left of this cavalry was a wood, in which they placed fome few battalions, and had begun to make an abattis, which was not compleated. From this defcription it appears, that the right and center were very ftrong, and fcarce to be attacked at all in front. The prince of Bevern, who, by taking that route, had put himfelf under the neceffity of fighting, in order to join M. Schwerin, had now no choice left but as to the manner of doing it: his corps was pofted

behind

behind a marshy rivulet, which, towards his left, ran so close to the enemy's line, that he could not pretend to pass it, and form under their fire; he therefore resolved to attack the enemy's left; and sent general Leftewitz over the Neifs, to attack, or rather amuse, their right. Things being thus concerted, he ordered his cavalry to advance and attack that of the enemy; this was executed with great bravery, but without success; they were repulsed every time; no wonder! because, in advancing towards the enemy, their left flank was exposed to the fire of the artillery of the redoubts, and that of the infantry behind them; and their right to that of the infantry posted, as we have said, in the wood, to the left of the enemy's horse. The prince, perceiving, at last, it would be in vain to renew the attack, while the enemy's horse was thus protected by the infantry and artillery on both flanks, ordered it back, and at the same time sent several battalions from his right, as high as was possible into the mountain, in order to come on the flank and rear of those which the enemy had posted in the wood, at the foot of it: this was punctually executed; the enemy abandoned the wood, and gave the prince's cavalry an opportunity to renew their attack, which must naturally succeed; that of the enemy, being unable to bear its shock, and the fire of the Prussian infantry, which had now got possession of the wood on their flank. On the retreat of the Austrian cavalry, the prince ordered his whole right to advance, and occupy the ground they had quitted; so that he was on and behind the enemy's left wing, and had, besides, the advantage of the rising ground, from whence he could with ease rake them from the left to the right. In this situation nothing remained for the Austrians to do, but to retire as soon as possible, for fear the enemy should push on towards Liebenau, and cut them off intirely; whch he might do, as, in pursuing the left wing, some of his troops were already behind them. The retreat was made in good order: count Lacy, who commanded the right, covered it; at Liebenau they took a new pofition, where they were reinforced by fome troops, who, on the march of prince Bevern, had quitted the frontiers, and fallen back to join the main body under count Kónigfeg.

Thus ended the combat of Reichenberg, in which the Auftrians loft one general, and about 1000 men killed, wounded, and taken; befides fome cannon left at Reichenberg. The lofs of the Pruffians was not much inferior.

Reflections.

As the only object the prince of Bevern could have in view, was to join M. Schwerin, we cannot conceive why he fhould march by Kratzau and Reichenberg, where the road is much more difficult than that by Gabel and Böhmifch Aycha, which was equally proper to effectuate his junction with Schwerin; and, moreover, was guarded only by fome light troops, at Gabel, which he might force, or leave behind, as he pleafed, without any difficulty or rifk. In taking this laft road, he was certainly at liberty to avoid an action; and, if the enemy remained at Reichenberg, he might find twenty pofitions behind them, and hinder them from retiring to Prague. It is always a great fault to fight, when nothing can be got by it; as in this cafe. The prince wanted to join Schwerin; he might have done it without fighting, and he could obtain no more by a fuccefsful action, as appears from the fact itfelf. He forced the enemy to quit their camp at Reichenberg; they took another at Liebenau, which he could not have forced, in all probability: he muft therefore have remained in the mountains, without any poffibility of joining Schwerin, if the march of this general had not determined count Kónigfeg to quit

quit Liebenau and retire. All which seems to prove, that the prince engaged in an action without any kind of reason, and from which he could not reap any advantage, whatever was the event. An immoderate desire of acquiring glory, makes men sometimes undertake things without sufficiently weighing the consequences. In the action he seems likewise to have been guilty of some faults: he formed parallel to the enemy, whose line could not be attacked, with any probability of success, excepting on the left; which, being once beat, the rest could not keep their ground; yet the prince did not reinforce his right, but left his troops nearly equally distributed throughout the whole line: his left, towards the Neiss, where it could be of no use at all, was as strong as where he formed his attack.

His attack with the cavalry was certainly ill-advised; for, though it succeeded, he could not prosecute his advantages; for, while the enemy had infantry in the wood, and their center kept its position, his cavalry could not occupy the ground on which that of the enemy stood. From the beginning he should have formed his right as high up the mountains as possible; brought the greatest part of his infantry there; and have done then what he was forced to do at last. The taking such a position would have forced the enemy to retire without fighting. His sending general Lestewitz to attack the enemy's right was needless. By occupying the wood, and part of the hill, on his right, the action was won; and all the manœuvres the enemy could make, on their right and center, would have been fruitless.

The Austrians camp seems, from our description of it, very strong; yet, on examination, it will be found otherwise; because the whole was not equally so; and therefore, properly speaking, no part of it. The right and center were strong by nature and art; being, as was said, fortified with redoubts, &c. but, as the left

left was weak, they could reap no benefit from them; unless they supposed the enemy so ignorant as to attack them there. From the general position of the ground, it was evident, that, if the left was forced to retire, the enemy, by occupying it, would be in the rear of the center and right, and force them to quit their advantageous position, and fall back instantly towards Johannisthal, for fear of being cut off from Liebenau: on this point, to their left, depended, no doubt, the success of the action. They should, consequently, have sent some of their best infantry into the wood on their left, and have placed some heavy artillery at the skirts of it; which, with that they had already, in the redoubts before their center, would have made it impossible for the enemy to pass the village of Bartzdorff, and the marshy rivulet they had before their front; much less form on this side of the rivulet. The Austrians could bring, against that point of attack, their artillery, their infantry, and their cavalry, to sustain them. In such circumstances prince Bevern could not certainly have formed his attack at all.

When the Austrians saw the enemy prepare to attack their left, why not make a general motion on that side, and carry their line up into the mountain? This manœuvre would have decided the action in their favour; and, by neglecting it, they were beat.

Their cavalry was too far advanced; which deprived them, in some measure, of the advantage of their artillery on the right, and of the infantry on the left, in the wood.

They should not have posted their whole army in the valley; for, though the mountains which formed it, seemed impassable; yet it happened otherwise: for the Prussian infantry did march through that on the left; gained the higher ground; and forced, consequently, the Austrians to abandon the wood at the foot of it. No corps whatever must be placed in a valley, unless you are masters of the mountains which form it; and, if you cannot occupy

occupy both fides, you muft, at leaft, one: for, though at firft fight, mountains, rocks, and woods, may appear impaffable; yet, upon a diligent inquiry, the contrary will be always found: for, in every country that is well peopled, there are, and muft be, communications between the villages; at leaft, for infantry: you muft, therefore, occupy the mountains and woods with your infantry; the valley underneath with your cavalry; which will hinder any enemy from paffing through it. From all which, it appears, that it was a bad camp, and a bad pofition; becaufe, having neglected to occupy the mountains, it could not be defended; and the troops, pofted in the valley, were not only expofed to be defeated, but likewife to be cut off from Prague, and their magazine at Buntzlaw, either by the prince of Bevern's corps, or by that of marfhal Schwerin.

The prince of Bevern marched, on the 23d, towards Liebenau; where, as we have faid, he found the enemy fo advantageoufly pofted, that he did not think it prudent to attack them: and the lefs fo, as he knew the march of Schwerin's corps would neceffarily force them to retire.

This laft general affembled his army, on the 18th of April, at Trautenau; from whence he marched, on the 19th, to Konigfhoff, where he paffed the Elbe. His intentions were to proceed towards Turnau and Liebenau, in order to facilitate the march of prince Bevern's corps; and, being joined with it, go to Prague. This plan was founded on the fame principles as that of the king's. Whatever troops the Auftrians might fend on the frontiers of Luface, they could not remain there, even though they had beat the duke of Bevern; becaufe the march of Schwerin, behind them, muft force them to retire, for fear of being taken between two fires; as it really happened: for, on the 24th, they quitted their camp at Liebenau, and marched with precipitation towards

Brandeifs;

Brandeifs; and from thence to Prague, where they arrived the 3d of May. M. Schwerin, in the mean time, marched from Königshoff to Giltchin, where he was informed of the action of Reichenberg, and of the enemy's retreat. Upon which he wifely changed his route, and marched on the Ifer; hoping still to cut them off from Prague: and, though he did not fucceed in this, he arrived at Jungbuntzlau, in time to feize an immenfe magazine which they had formed there.

Having been joined by the prince of Bevern's corps, he proceeded to Brandeifs; where he continued 'till the 4th of May: then he paffed the Elbe, and encamped on the other fide, not thinking it prudent to advance 'till he had concerted meafures with the king.

His majefty, having thrown a bridge over the Moldau, near Podbaba, paffed that river, with part of his army, on the 5th; leaving the remainder, under marfhal Keith, on the Weiffenberg. The 6th, at 5 in the morning, marfhal Schwerin's army arrived; and, having reconnoitred the enemy, the whole marched on the left, and foon after the battle begun. We will give here the different relations, that were publifhed by authority, of this memorable action.

That publifhed at Vienna is as follows:

" His royal highnefs prince Charles of Lorrain was informed,
" on the 4th of May, that the king of Pruffia had thrown bridges
" over the Moldau, near Roftock and Podbaba, in order to join
" M. Schwerin's army, by Winorz, and then attack our right,
" or cut off the communication with our magazines at Kollin and
" Kuttenberg. His royal highnefs changed his pofition fo, that
" the left came to the town of Prague, and the right towards
" Malefchitz and Biechowitz. The 5th the Pruffians vanguard
" paffed the Moldau: we ordered feveral batteries to be raifed
" before

" before the front of our army: at 11 o'clock, in the night, the
" king ordered his whole army to pafs that river, leaving only a
" fmall corps, and a great quantity of artillery, on the Weiffenberg.
" The junction of his, and Schwerin's army, was made on the
" 6th, at break of day. Immediately afterwards the whole Pruf-
" fian army, amounting to above 100,000 men, advanced againft
" us. M. Schwerin ordered the left wing, which he commanded,
" to attack our right, and endeavour to break it; while the king
" alarmed our left. His royal highnefs prince Charles of Lorrain,
" whofe army confifted of 55,000 only, faw himfelf obliged, by
" the motions of M. Schwerin, to order his fecond line to enter
" into the firft, and place it fo as to cover the right wing; the
" left being already covered by the cannon of Prague. His royal
" highnefs left only two regiments of horfe there, and placed the
" other thirteen, in three lines, on our right, the better to fuftain
" it. All thefe motions were made according as the Pruffians
" extended themfelves, in order to take us in flank; which
" M. Schwerin had principally in view. We occupied feveral
" heights; and M. Schwerin had likewife fome before him, which
" he muft occupy before he could approach us. Our artillery
" began to fire about 7 o'clock; which, as well as that of the
" infantry, produced fo great an effect, that the whole line of
" M. Schwerin, which, according to the report of the deferters,
" had orders to attack us, with their bayonnets fixed, was totally
" overthrown: while our cavalry attacked Schwerin's; beat it
" back three times; and difperfed it. As the Pruffians firft line
" was thrown back in confufion on the fecond, this fired upon
" them, and marched over their dead and wounded companions
" towards us. They were, however, received as the firft time,
" and again beat back. Our right wing, profiting of their victory,
" followed the flying enemy, in good order, above 600 paces;
" took

" took several pair of colours; 16 pieces of cannon; and a great
" number of prisoners. Our right, having thus advanced, left
" a great opening between it and the left. The king of Prussia
" marched, in the greatest haste, with several columns, and occu-
" pied this vacant space; and, at the same time, ordered a fresh
" body of horse to advance, full gallop, and occupy the ground
" where his left had stood, and thereby come behind our right,
" which was pursuing the enemy; so that this right wing, which
" had been victorious for three hours, was of a sudden surrounded
" by the enemy: and, to augment our misfortunes, there raised
" such a cloud of dust, as hindered us from knowing each other;
" and such a confusion ensued, that it was impossible for us to
" assemble the men, and put them again in order. Part of our
" infantry did, however, all that was possible to join our left
" wing; in which they succeeded; and retired, step by step, under
" a continual fire, to Prague; where they entered together. Two
" thousand of our right wing stopped near the field of battle, and
" thereby sustained the rest of the troops that were in confusion.
" All our artillery of reserve, the heavy baggage, pontoons, mili-
" tary chest, and 16000 men from our right wing, assembled, the
" 8th, at Benefchau. In two days 3000 Prussian deserters are
" come to the army, who all declare, that the Prussians have lost,
" killed, wounded, and missing, above 20,000 men. In dead,
" and wounded, we have lost, at most, 4000 men; and 2500
" taken prisoners; and no more than 20 field pieces are lost.
" During the battle, major general Beck, with a corps of Croats,
" attacked the town of Brandeifs, sword in hand; beat a Prussian
" battalion, that was there in garrison, of which he killed 100 men;
" and, after he had broke the bridge over the Elbe, retired with 5
" pair of colours, 2 cannon, 500 horses, a rich booty, and 678
" prisoners, among whom was the lieutenant colonel Mardefeld,
                                                            " and

" and all the officers of the battalion who were alive; all which
" he brought to M. Daun's camp. On our side M. Brown was
" wounded. On that of the Prussians M. Schwerin, and five or
" six other generals, are killed; and general Winterfield mortally
" wounded."

The Prussians account of this battle is as follows:

" The king joined M. Schwerin's army the 6th of May, in
" the morning; and it was resolved to attack the enemy imme-
" diately. The imperial army was encamped, with the left, on
" the Ziskaberg; and the right, on a hill, near Sterboholi. It
" was determined to attack the enemy's right; the Prussian army,
" therefore, marched, on the left, through the village of Pots-
" chernitz. M. Brown, having observed this motion, ordered
" his army to march on the right, that he might not be taken
" in flank. The Prussians were obliged to pass through some
" hollow ways, and over some marshy ground, on the other side
" of the village of Bischowitz, which threw the infantry into
" some disorder; and, the attack having been made in too much
" haste, they were repulsed. Marshal Schwerin, the greatest
" general of his time, was killed, with the colours in his hands,
" at the head of his own regiment. As soon as our infantry was
" formed again, they renewed the attack against the enemy's
" right wing. Prince Henry, the king's brother, alighted from
" his horse, and put himself at the head of his brigade; with
" which he mounted, or rather climbed up the mountains; and,
" having beat off the enemy, took several batteries. The cavalry
" of our left wing, after three attacks, forced that of the Austrians
" to retire. Our center, in the same manner, beat the enemy's
" infantry, and pursued them through their camp, which was
" still standing. Our left wing, to which some cavalry was
" joined, marched to Michele; and we separated the Austrian
" army; the right wing of which fled to the Zassava. Upon
" which

History of the War

"which our right attacked the enemy's left, and took succeſſively
"three batteries, placed on the hills. Our right wing of horſe had
"no opportunity to come to action. Prince Ferdinand of Brunſ-
"wic attacked the enemy's left in flank; and, as the king, with
"his left, and a body of horſe, had already reached the Moldau,
"all the Auſtrian infantry was forced to throw themſelves into
"Prague. They attempted to march out, on the ſide of König-
"ſaal, but were drove back by M. Keith's corps. We have taken
"above 4000 priſoners; among whom are 30 officers: beſides
"60 cannon, and 10 ſtandards. On our ſide we have loſt, 3099
"men, 54 officers, 340 horſes, killed: 8208 men, 397 officers,
"and 246 horſes, wounded: and 1557 men, 6 officers, miſſing."
Among the dead were M. Schwerin,* and major general Amſtel.
Among

---

* M. Schwerin was born the 26th of October, 1684. He ſtudied at Leiden, Roſtock, and Greifswalde. In 1699 he ſerved in a Dutch regiment belonging to his uncle; in 1705 he had a company. His uncle having quitted the Dutch ſervice, he did the ſame; in 1706 was made a lieutenant colonel in the duke of Mecklenburg's ſervice; in 1707 a colonel. The duke Charles Leopold ſent him in 1712 to the king of Sweden, Charles the 12th, at Bender; with whom he continued a year. On his return he was made a brigadier; and in 1718 a major general; in 1719 he commanded the Mecklenburg troops, at the battle of Walmſmoelen, againſt the Commiſſion's army, and beat them: and, the duke having reformed the greateſt part of his troops, the marſhal entered into the Pruſſian ſervice as major general; in 1723 he had a regiment given him; in 1724 was ſent as miniſter to the court of Poland; in 1730 was made governor of Peitz; in 1731 a lieutenant general; in 1732 knight of the black eagle; in 1739 general of infantry; in 1740 a field marſhal. He diſtinguiſhed himſelf much at the battle of Molwitz, the 16th of April, 1741; where he received two conſiderable wounds: in 1744 he marched with a great army into Bohemia; where he joined the king, at Prague, and commanded the ſiege of that place; where he diſtinguiſhed himſelf very much; in 1756 he commanded, as we have ſaid, the army in Sileſia; and, during that campaign, gave great proofs of his ſuperior abilities in the art of war; and was killed with the colours of his regiment in his hand. He was rather a little ſized man; he had, however, a martial look; loved the ſoldiers; and was very careful of them; and was therefore much beloved by them: and, though he on ſome occaſions was very hot, in all his expeditions he knew how to combine the greateſt bravery with the greateſt prudence. After the battle of Lowoſitz the king wrote to him to act cautiouſly (d'aller bride en main.) He was twice married, and has left children of both ſexes.

Among the wounded were lieutenant generals Fouquet, Hautcharmois, and Winterfield; and major generals Plettenberg, Schöning, and Blankenfee. Thefe two accounts of the battle are far from being clear and explicit, and give but a very confufed idea of the action. We fhall therefore add another, wrote by count Schwerin, general adjutant to the marfhal of that name, which feems to be, by far, the beft that appeared on that occafion.

" In confequence of the meafures concerted with M. Schwerin,
" his majefty paffed the Moldau, at Seltz, the 5th of May, 1757,
" at 8 o'clock in the morning, with the corps he propofed joining
" to the marfhal's army; of which he gave us notice, as had been
" agreed, by a twelve pound fhot, to which the marfhal anfwered
" with the fame fignal. At 2 o'clock in the evening his majefty
" fent Stutterheim, one of his adjutants, to the marfhal, with
" orders, that we, and the column commanded by general Win-
" terfield, fhould break up at 12 o'clock that night, and compafs
" our march, fo that the head of our columns fhould arrive, ex-
" actly at 4 in the morning, upon the heights of Brofiz, where
" his majefty promifed to be, on the right, by Tfchimniz. Thefe
" orders were executed with fuch precifion, that our three columns
" arrived, at the place of rendezvous, at 4 o'clock; and, at fuch
" a diftance from each other, as to leave only the fpace neceffary
" to form the line. We did not meet with any obftacle, on our
" march, 'till we came to the heights before Brofiz; where Mo-
" dena's regiment of horfe, two of dragoons, and Feftetitz's huf-
" fars, were pofted that night. Thefe fired upon our vanguard,
" and retired immediately, through Brofiz, to the left wing of
" their army.

" As foon as the king had wifhed the marfhal and general
" Winterfield a good morning, he rode, with thefe two generals,
" without any other efcort than two of his adjutants, captain
" Platen, lieutenant colonel Oelfnitz, and myfelf, to one of the
" higheft

" highest hills on the other side of Brosiz. From hence we could
" discover all the enemy's camp very plain; the first and second
" line from one end to the other. His majesty reconnoitred it
" with his spying glass. When the enemy perceived seven or
" eight persons on the hill, he sent us some four pounders, but
" without effect. His majesty continued above an hour here, to
" examine their position, and how they were to be attacked.
" The enemy was posted, with the left wing towards Prague,
" on the Ziskaberg, behind the Invalides: the right extended
" about 2000 paces beyond the village of Conradiz, near Ster-
" boholi. Two hundred paces before their front, the mountains
" were so steep and craggy, that no cavalry or artillery could pos-
" sibly ascend them. At the foot of these mountains is a deep
" valley, which was intirely occupied by some hussars and Hun-
" garian infantry. The mountains on our side of the valley were
" no less steep and craggy than the others: notwithstanding these
" difficulties, his majesty was inclined to attack the enemy in
" front. The marshal, on the contrary, represented to him the
" difficulty of the ground; the great march the troops had made;
" and the strength of the enemy's position; who had covered the
" heights before their front with a prodigious quantity of heavy
" artillery. His majesty, convinced by these reasons, permitted
" the marshal to go and seek out some more convenient place to
" form the attack. Upon which his excellency rode, full gallop,
" before the enemy's right, where the ground on both sides falls
" gradually, and where he perceived a plain, before the enemy's
" right wing, near the village of Miesiz, where the infantry could
" pass over the meadows, and the cavalry and heavy artillery over
" the damms. As soon as the marshal had reconnoitred the
" ground, and given an account of it to the king, orders were
" immediately given to the three corps to move on the left. This

" was

" was executed with such celerity, that the army, which had
" received the orders about nine o'clock, marched above four
" miles through very bad roads, and at half an hour past ten was
" formed; and at eleven the battle begun on the left wing. All
" our cavalry was passing the damm, when that of the Austrians
" first turned out, and formed itself in order of battle, without
" taking down one tent. They did not probably perceive that
" our intention was to attack their right flank, 'till they saw two
" regiments of our cavalry pass the damm, and form directly
" on it. This manœuvre drew their attention that way: they
" then ordered all their cavalry from the left; which, with great
" celerity, came and formed itself, on a fine plain, on the right,
" in 104 squadrons, in three lines, with intervals equal to the
" front of a squadron. This manœuvre was executed with such
" promptitude, that our lieutenant general, the hereditary prince
" of Schónaich, who had only 65 squadrons, fearing to be out-
" flanked, resolved instantly to attack the enemy, without waiting
" for the right wing which the king had ordered to come and
" reinforce him. Accordingly the attack was made in the best
" order. The enemy stood still 'till we came within 50 paces of
" them, then they fired their carabines; and at 30 they advanced
" with a strong pace against us. We were outwinged by 8 squa-
" drons, and therefore 'tis no wonder our cavalry had such a hard
" task, and was twice repulsed. In the third attack, Stechow's
" regiment of dragoons, commanded by colonel Winterfield, and
" general Ziethen, with 20 squadrons of Ziethen's and Putkam-
" mer's hussars, advanced with so much bravery, that not only
" the enemy's cavalry was intirely defeated, but part of it was
" pushed on their own grenadiers, on the right wing, which
" threw them back in the utmost confusion. During this attack of
" the cavalry, the grenadiers of our left wing, and the regiments

" of

" of Fouquet, Kreutzen, and Schwerin's infantry, having paſſed
" over ſome meadows, were forced to advance through a very
" narrow road, in order to join the reſt of the line, which was
" already formed. As ſoon as the grenadiers appeared on the
" other ſide of the defile, they were received with twelve poun-
" ders, charged with cartridges, in ſuch a manner, that they
" were inſtantly forced to retire, and quit the defile in the
" greateſt confuſion. In the mean time the enemy's fire grew
" ſtill more violent, and at laſt obliged the grenadiers to retire
" back over the damm. They were followed by Fouquet's and
" Kreutzen's regiments; and, as the ſecond battalion of Schwerin's
" begun to do the ſame, the marſhal, who had been continually
" on the other ſide of the defile, took the colours out of the
" officer's hands, and rode before the regiment; doing all that
" was poſſible to make them advance. He drew the troops, as
" well as he could, out of the defile; and, having put them again
" in order, advanced with a ſtrong pace towards the enemy.
" Scarce had he marched 12 ſteps, when he received ſeveral
" ſhot; one in the ear, another in the heart, and three in the
" body: he fell inſtantly from his horſe, without the leaſt ſigns
" of life. General Manteufel took the colours out of his hand,
" and gave them to the enſign; who had ſcarce received them,
" when a cannon ſhot came and killed him on the ſpot. Imme-
" diately after this the whole line advanced. Our artillery did
" great execution. The lines were at above 60 paces diſtant from
" each other; when the enemy's infantry, on the right, was ob-
" ſerved to be in the greateſt confuſion. Their center kept their
" ground much longer; being protected by a great quantity of
" artillery. His majeſty, obſerving that the enemy's right wing
" purſued our left with great vivacity, inſomuch that it was ſepa-
" rated from the reſt of the army, laid hold of this favourable
" opportunity;

" opportunity; and, with the greateft celerity, marched, with his
" right, to occupy the fpace which the enemy, by advancing,
" had left open: and, by this means, feparated the two wings
" from each other. Now the confufion was general in the ene-
" my's army. Our left wing, being again formed, attacked the
" purfuing enemy, and drove them back: and, when they endea-
" voured to retire to the army, they found the ground occupied
" by the king. His majefty ordered an attack to be made, with
" fixed bayonnets, on the enemy's left wing, that was likewife
" flying. Here a great carnage enfued; particularly in taking
" the redoubt; where the fecond battalion of prince Henry's did
" wonders. The enemy's left fled into Prague; and the right,
" in confufion, towards Malefchitz and Bifchowitz."

BEFORE we give an account of what followed this memorable battle, it is neceffary to examine the various operations which preceded it, as well as the conduct of the action itfelf, that the reader may be able to form a proper judgment of them, as they are in themfelves, and independant of the events. For thefe do not always proceed from fine difpofitions; nor are prudent and wife meafures conftantly attended with happy fucceffes. In general, however, it muft be confeffed, that few or no enterprizes fail, but by fome error, which might have been forefeen, and confequently avoided.

THE plan, formed by the Auftrians, to remain on the defenfive 'till their allies took the field, and thereby give them a favourable opportunity to act with vigour, was certainly wife and prudent: but they feem to have failed in the execution. Two thirds of the enemy's troops were cantoned in Saxony and Lufatia, and the remainder in the neighbourhood of this laft province; which indicated, very plainly, that, in cafe he propofed to invade Bohemia, it would be on that fide; particularly as the king was there in
perfon.

person. Besides, by entering Bohemia from the side of Saxony, this last would be covered by that very manœuvre: whereas, if it was done from Silesia, another army must be left to guard Saxony. They ought to have known the king better, than to suppose he would act with part of his forces only, when he had it in his power to do it with the whole. Moreover, if, contrary to all appearances, as well as to the nature of things, he attempted to invade Moravia, he could not, in less than a month, bring his armies on that side; and the Austrians did not require half that time to bring all their forces there. If his majesty sent a corps there only, the garrison of Olmutz, sustained by some Croats, a regiment of dragoons, and another of hussars, would have been sufficient to cover the country.

From all which, it appears, that the Austrians acted very imprudently, in posting a corps of above 20,000 men in Moravia, where they were quite useless. What augments this first fault, was the leaving it there even after the Prussian army was in motion, as well in Saxony and Lusatia, as about Schweidnitz; which demonstrated their intention was to penetrate that way into Bohemia.

This corps should, no doubt, have been placed, during the winter, so as to form a chain from Moravia to Königshoff; and, in the month of March, their quarters should have been drawn nearer each other; and the center placed about Pardubitz. This would have enabled them to assemble, on the least notice, either on the right, towards Leutomischel, or on the left, behind the Elbe, about Schurtz.

When the Prussians were in motion, this corps should have assembled at Schurtz; because, from thence, it was at hand to join count Königseg; and, being united, were much superior to the duke of Bevern's, or marshal Schwerin's; and therefore might

attack

attack either of these generals, if they presumed, which was not probable, to penetrate into Bohemia, and hinder them from joining their forces. But this was neglected, and the corps in Moravia quite forgot; as one may imagine: for, though the enemy had entered Bohemia at the other extremity, about the 20th of April, yet this corps, on the 6th of May, was only arrived at Böhmisch Brodt, within twenty miles of Prague. As to count Königseg's corps, it has been already observed, that it was posted too far in the mountains, and exposed to be taken in between the prince of Bevern's corps, and that of M. Schwerin.

THE Austrians committed the same fault exactly, in the distribution of their troops on the frontiers of Saxony.

IT was by no means probable, that the king would order a considerable corps to enter Bohemia, near Egra; because, being at so great a distance from his other columns, it would be exposed to be cut off by the superior forces of the Austrians; who must necessarily take a central position between that corps and the king's, as they had the greatest part of their forces in the circles of Saatz and Leutmeritz.

IT was still less probable the enemy would undertake any thing against Egra; which, if provided with a common garrison, cannot be taken without a siege; which most certainly he would not undertake, as it cannot, from its situation, facilitate the operations against Bohemia: and, if against all rules of war, he did lay siege to it, they might in four days have brought their army to its relief. From whence it appears evident, that the placing a corps in the neighbourhood of Egra was of no use, and subject to be cut off from the main army at Budyn, whenever the enemy entered Bohemia by the defiles of Kupferberg and Basberg; as it really happened: because M. Brown was forced to quit the position at Bduyn, in order to join the duke of Aremberg: whereas, if this general had taken a position at Commottau, with all his light troops, sustained by some battalions of good infantry, in the two last mentioned defiles, it is plain prince Maurice could not penetrate that way, as he did; and, though he had, he could not join the king until he beat the duke, who might have been sustained by the whole army under the marshal at Budyn. This last was likewise ill posted, being too far back to sustain any body of troops he might send to occupy the defiles beween Pirna and Lowositz; which we think is the only method that can effectually hinder an enemy that attempts to penetrate that way into Bohemia. The marshal ought, therefore, to have assembled his quarters beyond the Egra, in such a manner as to be able, in one march, to be behind the Bila at Auffig: from whence he might either sustain the light troops placed behind the ravin of Ghishubel, or, as he thought most convenient, let them fall back on his army, and defend the position at Auffig, which, if occupied by an army, cannot be forced. Even, perhaps, it would have been more advantageous to advance with the whole army, behind the ravin of Ghishubel, and have sent the duke of Aremberg, with his whole corps, into the mountains of Basberg; because these positions not only covered Bohemia, but also enabled the Austrians to penetrate into Saxony, if it was thought proper: whereas the different positions, taken by the Austrian army, in order to cover Bohemia, did not answer that end, and moreover exposed the different corps to be beat in detail, and hindered from joining each other; as it happened to that in Lusatia, under count Königseg; and that in Moravia, under marshal Daun; the first having been beat, and the other hindered from joining the rest of the troops at Prague. There is scarce any operation of war more delicate and difficult than the distribution of the troops into winter quarters: it requires a perfect knowledge of the country, and must be regulated by a

prodigious

prodigious variety of circumstances: 1. regard must be had to the enemy's disposition; 2. to his general plan of war, and to the particular object he has in view the ensuing campaign; 3. to the object you have yourself in view for the following campaign. If you propose to be on the defensive, the distribution of the troops must be made in such a manner as to be able to unite in different points, without leaving even a possibility of their being intercepted in their march to the place of rendezvous: that these points be chosen as near the frontiers as possible, in order to cover the country; and that they be so well chosen, that the enemy can neither force you in them, nor leave you behind. If you propose being on the offensive, the troops must be so distributed, that, in one march, or two, they form several great corps on the enemy's frontiers, and pass them so as to separate his quarters, and run no risk of being intercepted before they join, and form one body in the enemy's country. Above all things, care must be taken that they are not exposed to be inquieted, during the winter, which the troops must enjoy in peace and safety, as well to refresh themselves, as to form the recruits, &c.

It must be acknowledged that the king of Prussia excells in this, as in many other parts of war: no general has ever opened the different campaigns with more greatness or precision. His quarters were so disposed, that it was scarce possible, from thence, to guess at his intentions; as he could, seemingly, with equal facility, form very different enterprizes: from whence it always happened that he begun his operations with great views, celerity, and exactness: and, when his troops were attacked in their quarters, they always assembled in the places appointed, without ever having suffered any considerable loss; which is the more extraordinary, as he had very few light troops, especially in the beginning. His disciple, prince Ferdinand, has likewise shewn himself infinitely

superior

superior to all the French generals, in this point, as appeared evidently on every occasion.

The Austrians neglected all the rules abovementioned, and were therefore forced to abandon the country, in order to unite the different corps, and moreover exposed to be beat in detail; as we have seen.

Having at last assembled their army at Prague, they were at liberty to attack either the king or marshal Schwerin, who were separated by a great river, and a most difficult country for military operations. They were much superior to either, and therefore ought to have risked an action in those circumstances; otherwise it is in vain to make war. If they thought themselves unequal to the king, or Schwerin, separately, they should not, certainly, have fought them both when united. They should not have permitted the king to pass such a river as the Moldau, in a most difficult place, and within sight of their camp, and remain with a very inconsiderable body of troops, compared to theirs, a whole day and a night on the same side of the river. They ought, no doubt, to have attacked him, either before he passed, or after, before he joined M. Schwerin; or, if they chose rather to attack this last, they should have left 20 battalions on the heights of Brositz, opposite Potbaba, to hinder the king from passing, and march to Brandeifs, against Schwerin, without delay.

The enemy having joined all his forces the 6th in the morning, in their presence, and his leaving M. Keith on the other side of the Moldau, in the sight of Prague, indicated very plainly, he proposed bringing things to an issue there. The Austrians should not therefore have been so confident in their numbers, and position, as to send their cavalry to forage, while the enemy was actually making some motions in their presence.

When

When they saw the enemy march on his left, they certainly did right to change their position; but this was only part of what they should have done. They ought to have brought all the artillery possible to bear against the village of Podschernitz, and have attacked him as he was advancing in columns through that village, and over the meadows, without giving him time, or ground to form upon. They should have put their horse in two close lines, which would have enabled them to extend their right quite up to the fishponds, which covered their flank effectually, and deprived the enemy of the ground, on which only he could form his cavalry; and, if they kept back their center a little, so as to form a curve, concave towards the enemy, which they certainly might have done, their right being covered by the ponds, and their left by the artillery and infantry of the right wing, in this case, the enemy could not advance at all, without presenting his left flank; which must always be decisive in every action, and particularly in cavalry. But the Austrians neglected all these precautions, and moreover suffered the enemy's horse, though less numerous, to take them in flank; and were consequently defeated. When M. Brown repulsed and pursued the enemy, he ought not to have broke the line, and rushed forward, like a young soldier, who sees and observes only what passes directly before him, without attending to the whole; and thereby regulate this or that particular manœuvre. When he advanced, he should have ordered the whole line to make the same motion; and, if he did not choose to quit the heights, where his center and left stood, he should have advanced his right, so as to form an oblique line with the right forwards. By this manœuvre, he was at liberty to bring all his reserve, and the right of the second line, to sustain the point of attack on which the victory depended; and, by keeping the line close, gave the enemy no advantage, how much soever he advanced;

with

with his right to purfue them to Podfchernitz. Even this oblique formation neceffarily enabled him to take the enemy's whole line in flank, and rake it from one end to the other. The marfhal, by advancing with the right only, broke the line, and thereby left an opening, which the enemy occupied, cut the army in two, and defeated it.

There is in every camp a certain point, which may very properly be called, the key of it, and on which depends the fuccefs of an action; while you keep this, the enemy has nothing; and when you lofe it, all is loft. The talent of finding out this point, is perhaps the moft fublime, and the moft rare, of any in the whole art of war. On this talent depends the fcience of camps, and the methods of attacking and defending them. In the prefent cafe, this point was, no doubt, that fpace of ground between the point of the right wing of infantry, and the pond near Sterboholi, where the cavalry fhould have been pofted, as it is marked in the plan, with the light troops and fome regular infantry in Sterboholi, and a battery on the height, before the right wing of horfe. While the Auftrians occupied this ground, they could not be defeated; but they had ftudied fo little the fcience of camps, that they did not perceive this point, and formed their cavalry a great way behind it; and were beat.

From all the preceding remarks, it appears, that M. Brown either did not know the country, or did not know how to occupy it properly, in the diftribution of his army into winter quarters; and that he committed numberlefs faults, as well before, as during the action; which neceffarily were followed with the lofs of it. As we know that he was a good foldier, and by no means a contemptible general, it is far from being impoffible, that fome private motives might make him lefs careful and clear-fighted than is confiftent with a perfon of his genius. He was, no doubt, little
pleafed

pleafed to fee prince Charles at the head of the army; and, being under the command of another, was, probably, lefs anxious about the event. Had he been alone, perhaps he would have acted otherwife. This fhews, how imprudent it is to employ, together, men whofe private views of ambition can fcarce ever coincide.

As to the king's difpofitions, they will, no doubt; appear very fine to thofe who are not fufficiently acquainted with the nature of military operations, or who have not attended to the defcription we have given of the country wherein thefe tranfactions happened. Events, like an impetuous torrent, hurry people away, without giving them time to reflect on their caufes, or examine the various circumftances which contributed to produce them; and therefore their opinion of things is feldom eftablifhed on clear and exact ideas.

BEING feparated from the enemy by a chain of mountains, and moreover protected by many ftrong places, he could diftribute his troops into winter quarters as he pleafed, without any rifk; becaufe the nature of the country enabled him to affemble them, before any confiderable body of the enemy could penetrate. The difpofition of his march into Bohemia, was fubject to a prodigious number of obftacles; many of which were, at leaft might have been, infurmountable.

PRINCE Maurice's column was feparated from that under the king by an interval of 50 miles; and, moreover, by a moft difficult country, full of mountains, woods, ravins, defiles, &c. The enemy had, in this very fpace of ground, an army much fuperior to either prince Maurice's, or the king's; they might confequently have taken forty pofitions that would have effectually hindered their junction; and, if they prefumed to advance one ftep into the country, attack either of them feparaetly; and, being much fuperior, probably defeat them.

EVEN

Even after their junction, M. Brown, with the duke of Aremberg, was still equal to them, and might have taken several positions between the Egra and Prague, which would have hindered them from approaching the Moldau, and joining Schwerin. Being at last assembled at Prague, they might have attacked either the king or Schwerin, with forces much superior to either. As these were separated by the Moldau, they might have been hindered from joining at all. When the king passed that river, leaving M. Keith* on the other side, the enemy were at liberty to destroy either of them, having more time than was necessary for that purpose. The same reasoning holds good with regard to the other two columns under prince Bevern and marshal Schwerin. They were so far separated, that the enemy might have taken such positions as would have hindered them from joining; and might, with superior forces, have attacked either. From whence it appears, that the king, by thus separating his columns at such an immense distance, exposed them to be beat in detail, and his whole army to destruction. His passing such a river as the Moldau, in sight of an immense army, his staying eighteen hours, at least, with a handful of men, in their presence, ought to have been fatal to him; and, if it happened otherwise, he must thank his good fortune.

* Marshal Keith, knight of the black eagle, of St. Andreas, and Alexander Newski's orders in Russia, was born of the illustrious family of Marshall, in Scotland. In 1730 he was a major general in Russia; in 1734 a lieutenant general, and went with the Russian troops into Germany; in 1737 he served against the Turks, and distinguished himself greatly at the taking of Oczakow, where he was wounded; in 1741 and 1742 he commanded against the Swedes, and got the battle of Williamstrand; in 1747 he quitted the Russian service, and entered that of Prussia; in 1749 was made knight of the black eagle, and governor of Berlin, with a pension of 12,000 dollars, besides his pay. He was killed in 1758, at the battle of Hochkirchen, at the head of the Prussian infantry, who had repulsed the Austrians, and were pursuing them. He was middle sized; had a very martial countenance; and was an humane and benevolent man.

His attacking the enemy in such a strong camp, and in the neighbourhood of a fortress, was certainly very rash, because it was very improbable that he beat them: and, though he did, he could not reap any great advantage from it; as they could always retire into Prague, and from thence march instantly out, and destroy marshal Keith in his presence, even after he had separated the two wings. 'Tis, in general, very imprudent to attack an army near a fortress; because, in case of success, 'tis impossible to proceed with cavalry, which alone can destroy a defeated army; whatever advantages the infantry may gain, they cannot prosecute them with such vigour and celerity, as to hinder an enemy from making a retreat, and get soon together again. Had the king got such a battle, 20 miles from any fortress, the whole Austrian army would have been destroyed. He was the less obliged to attack the enemy in this position, as, by directing his march towards Kollin and Kuttenburg, where the enemy had their magazines, they would have followed him, and given him a more favourable opportunity to attack them; and, in all probability, he would have met M. Daun, then coming from Moravia, whom he might have crushed. This manœuvre would have enabled him to destroy the enemy's magazines, and force them to fight on his own terms, or submit to be cut off from Vienna. As to the action itself, he had no choice in his attack; it could be done only on the left; but his seeing, and seizing the critical and decisive moment that M. Brown gave him, by breaking his line, is such a stroke of superior genius, that few, very few, are capable of. His prudence, in re-establishing the line, continually, as he advanced, and his whole conduct during the action, most justly deserve the greatest approbation. What appears rash in the manœuvres which immediately preceded it, must, probably, be attributed to the necessity of his affairs, and to the knowledge he had of thofe generals who oppofed him. His majefty feems too great a general to commit a common fault.

Prince Charles, with near 50,000 men, having been forced to throw himfelf into Prague, the king formed the extraordinary project of blockading him in that place. As it is very populous, the addition of near 60,000 men, including fervants, and the followers of the army, would, he hoped, foon force them to furrender for want of fubfiftence.

During this celebrated blockade, nothing happened, but what is common; and therefore, we think, a detail of the operations would be no lefs infipid, than ufelefs. In fuch an operation of war, nothing more is to be done, than to occupy fuch pofts, in the neighbourhood of the place, as moft effectually prevent any fuccours, provifions, or intelligence, to enter. Thofe who are fhut up, on the contrary, endeavour to open the chain as often as poffible, that their wants may be relieved. The nature of the ground, the number and fpecies of the troops on each fide, are the only matters to be confulted, as to the methods to be ufed on thefe occafions: no rule can be given as to the manner of occupying properly a piece of ground; genius alone can do it, and precepts are vain.

It is, no doubt, a thing worthy remark, and will appear a fable to pofterity, that near 50,000 men, with a train of artillery, arms, &c. fhould fubmit to be fhut up for fix weeks, and reduced to extremity, by an army of equal force. That of the king did not certainly, at the end of May, exceed that of the Auftrians; which will appear evident, if we confider how many men he had loft in the battle, by ficknefs, defertion, and the numberlefs detached corps. This army, fmall as it was, formed a chain of pofts, which extended many miles, and was moreover feparated by the Moldau; over which they communicated by two bridges only;

the

the one above, and the other below the town: fo that, in fact, the Auftrians, had they chofe to march out of the place, would have had no more than half the Pruffian army to contend with: why therefore they did not, no man, that has the leaft idea of military affairs, can ever comprehend. A torrent carried one of the bridges away; yet did they continue quiet, and let flip this favourable opportunity, without making any attempt to go out. We have been very often on the ground about Prague, and muft own, it is, and will be, a matter of wonder and aftonifhment, that no effort was made to march out. Had they attacked the Pruffians, thus feparated by a great river, and divided into fo many fmall detachments, they could not fail in their attempt; they muft have deftroyed their army. It is no lefs furprizing, that fo great a general as the king of Pruffia fhould think it poffible to reduce an army of 50,000 men, in fuch an extenfive town as Prague, with one of equal force. The fupinenefs of the Auftrians juftified this attempt, and faved his army from inevitable deftruction.

WHEN the king fummoned prince Charles to furrender, marfhal Brown, then fick in bed, being confulted, anfwered, with no lefs fpirit than amazement, " Eft ce que fa majefté croit que nous "fommes tous des C—ll—ns. Dites au prince que mon avis eft, " que fon alteffe aille fur le champ attaquer le M. Keith."

THE celebrated marfhal Belleifle, who knew Prague perfectly well, had, in the preceding war, with 15,000 men, defended it for many months againft the Auftrians; and, being at laft reduced to the greateft extremity, quitted it with 12,000 men, and retired to Egra, with fafety and glory. This general wrote a letter, while the king was blockading that town; which I have feen; wherein he fays, " Je connois Prague, fi j'y etois, avec la moitié des " troupes, que le prince Charles y a actuéllement je detruirois " l'armée Pruffienne."

WHILE the king was occupied before Prague, he sent out several detachments, in order to raise contributions, and secure, or destroy, the magazines which the enemy had formed in different parts of Bohemia. General Oldenbourg and colonel Meyer were sent into the empire with the same view, and to hinder, or at least retard, the operations of the army of the empire. But all their operations are of too insignificant a nature to deserve any particular detail; none of them had, nor indeed could have, any considerable influence on the general plan of operations. We shall therefore pass them in silence.

MARSHAL Daun, who now commanded the army in Moravia, which had been the preceding campaign under the orders of prince Piccolomini, having received orders to join the main army at Prague, quitted Moravia, and directed his march for that purpose. However, on the 6th of May, he was only arrived at Böhmisch Brodt, within 12 miles of that place, where he was informed of the battle. He continued here for some days, and then retired to Kollin, as well to avoid an action, as to join the right wing, which, as we have already said, had retired to Benefchau.

THE king, fearing that this army, which amounted to above 40,000 men, might not only disturb his operations before Prague, but likewise, by some manœuvre or other, give prince Charles an opportunity to get out of that place, thought it necessary to drive them further back. For which purpose, the prince of Bevern, with about 25,000 men, was ordered to execute this plan.

As this general advanced, the marshal very wisely retired, in order to receive the reinforcements which were in march to join him, and fell back successively to Kollin, Kuttenberg, Goltzjenkau, and Haber.

HAVING

HAVING at length received all the reinforcements, artillery, &c. which he expected, he gave orders, the 11th of June in the evening, to march next morning. Accordingly the army quitted the camp of Jenikau the 12th, and marched the same day to Janovitzy. The next day general Nadafti was attacked at Pikan; but, being fuftained by the whole army, the Pruffians were repulfed with lofs. This general, having been reinforced, was ordered to march by Malefchau, and take poft at Suchdol, while general Beck, with about 6000 men, was commanded to occupy Kuttenberg; which the Pruffians had quitted on the 12th, and retired to Kollin. On the 14th the marfhal marched to Gintitz, and on the 16th to Krichenau, where he encamped as in A. A. This whole march was conducted with much prudence and vigour; infomuch that the enemy was more than once on the point of being attacked, and probably defeated; being much inferior. The marfhal, by the direction of his march, feems to have intended to bring prince Bevern to an action before he was joined by any reinforcements, or to have cut him off from Prague; the difficulty of the roads and the good conduct of the prince prevented it.

THE king, being informed of the enemy's approach, quitted his army before Prague on the 13th, and marched towards Kollin; where he propofed uniting the feveral corps, he had detached, to the army under prince Bevern, and then attack the enemy without delay. On the 14th he marched by Schwartz Kofteletz, and Zdanitz, intending to encamp at Malotitz; but, on approaching that place, a large body of troops was difcovered marching behind Zafmuck. Being no ways prepared for an action, having only a few battalions with him, his majefty threw them into the village of Zdanitz, with the cavalry on the plain before it, and continued in this pofition 'till he was joined by the different detachments he expected.

THE

The camp occupied by the enemy, at Krichenau, was judged too advantageous to be attacked in front, with any probability of success: nor could it be approached on the left, without marching, a great way up, to the source of the ravin which covered it. This would give the marshal time to change his position, as he thought most convenient, and perhaps afford him an opportunity to give the king the slip, and march to Prague. For which reason his majesty resolved to occupy the hills of Chotzemitz, behind the enemy's right. Accordingly, on the 18th in the morning, the army was ordered to march on its left, along the great road that goes from Prague towards Kollin. During the march, advice was brought that the enemy was retiring; which was soon found to be a mistake; for he had only changed his position, and was observed to be putting his army in order of battle, on the very ground which the king proposed to occupy.

The marshal, seeing the enemy's army move on its left, easily perceived the king's intentions were to attack him on his right flank: to avoid which, he ordered his army to move on the right, first to B. B. the reserve in D. D. then to G. G. with the reserve in E. E. and general Nadasti's corps in F. F. His army, consisting of 60,000 men, was formed in two lines; the infantry on the wings, and the cavalry in the center. The right of the infantry was posted on a high hill, quite close to an open wood occupied by the light troops. At a small distance before the front was the village of Krzeczor, in which some battalions were placed very properly, as they could with ease be sustained by the line. The hill, on which this village stands, presents, towards the right, very high and steep precipices, which cannot be passed by any species of troops. At the bottom of this hill is another village, which was likewise occupied by some infantry. Out of the hill, a little behind this last village, runs a rivulet almost perpendicular to the

enemy's

enemy's line; the banks of it are very high and craggy. Behind this rivulet Nadafti's corps was at firft placed, and then in F. F. fo that the enemy could not advance to attack the line, without prefenting his flank to this corps. On the left of Krzeczor, on a high and fteep hill, is the village of Brzift, a little before the line, alfo occupied by fome infantry. The left was likewife on a very high hill, which commands all the plain about it. Near the left is the village of Podhorz; through which runs a marfhy rivulet, which effectually covered that wing. All the ground before the front was very unequal; this obliges a line, marching to attack it, to ftop often, in order to clofe and form again; which is a great difadvantage, particularly being near the enemy, whofe artillery cannot fail doing great execution.

The king ordered his army to halt in the plain near Siatiflunz and Novimiefto, while he reconnoitred the enemy's pofition; whom, notwithftanding the ftrength of it, he refolved to attack. The army was again put in motion, and foon after the battle begun: of which we fhall give the different relations that were publifhed. By which means the reader will be enabled to form a proper judgment of this great and decifive action. The firft is that publifhed by the court of Vienna; the fecond is that of the Pruffians; and the laft, which is more extenfive than the others, was wrote by a French officer, who was at the Auftrian army by order of his court.

" As foon as the imperial and royal army quitted the camp of
" Gintitz, on the 16th of June in the evening, in order to oc-
" cupy that which had been marked out at Krichenau, his Pruf-
" fian majefty quitted likewife that of Kaurzim, and pofted his
" army on the heights behind Planian. Upon which the Auftrian
" army changed its pofition that fame evening, and was pofted, in
" order of battle, between two heights, that were to the right
" and

" and left. On the 18th, in the morning, the enemy marched
" towards Planian, and halted between that place and the Inn
" called Slatiflunz. At 1 o'clock, however, his army was put
" again in motion, in four columns. As soon as his excellency
" marshal Daun perceived that the enemy's intention was to come
" on his right flank, he ordered the reserve, and all the second
" line, to march there, and form a flank to cover the right wing.
" General Nadasti, with his hussars and Croats, was likewise or-
" dered there for the same purpose. The first line continued in
" its first position 'till the enemy's left wing was seen to advance,
" in several columns, against the flank and right wing of the
" Austrian army; then it was ordered to march on its right,
" quite close to the abovementioned flank; and, at two in the
" evening, it was at length formed upon the heights. Then the
" heavy artillery, on both sides, began to play. The enemy's at-
" tack on our right wing was so violent, that it threw the cavalry
" into confusion: it was, however, put again in order, by the
" bravery and good conduct of the generals Serbelloni, Daun,
" Odonell, Trautmansdorff, and Aspremont; and then they re-
" pulsed the Prussians. Notwithstanding which, the enemy ad-
" vanced on the heights of the village of Krzeczor, still nearer
" our flank. As soon as they reached the village, they burnt it;
" which was the signal to their right wing to attack our left. At
" half an hour after three they made a most violent attack on our
" flank, and immediately after on our right and left wing. Some
" hundred men, formed in half a square, penetrated through the
" flank; they were, however, drove back by our cavalry and the
" Saxon carabineers. The enemy renewed his attacks seven dif-
" ferent times; in each of which he was repulsed; and at last
" forced to abandon us a compleat victory. Upon which the
" Austrian army took its third position on the heights, where it
" remained

" remained all night, in order of battle; and, on the 19th, retired
" to the old camp of Krichenau. During the action, the king was
" on a hill behind his left wing, from whence he gave his orders.
" The enemy, in their retreat, burnt the villages of Brzafam and
" Kutliers: their left wing went towards the village of Welin;
" and their right towards Nimburg. This battle, which lafted
" from 2 o'clock 'till nine, may be reckoned among the moft re-
" markable and bloody that have happened for a long time. It
" was conducted, on both fides, with no lefs valour than pru-
" dence; 'till the Pruffians were, at length, thrown into the
" greateft confufion, and forced to take a precipitate flight, by
" two different ways, and in fmall divifions; as chance brought
" them together. Their lofs, on this occafion, may be certainly
" reckoned at 20,000 men: 6500 were found dead on the field
" of battle; and above 7000 prifoners: among which are lieu-
" tenant general Trefkow, major general Pannewitz, and 120 ftaff
" officers; befides 3000 deferters. We have taken 22 pair of
" colours, and 45 pieces of cannon. The lofs of the Auftrian
" army amounts to above 6000 men, killed, wounded, and mif-
" fing. Among the firft is lieutenant general Lutzow; and among
" the fecond were count Serbelloni, general of horfe, lieutenant
" general Wolwart, and major generals prince Lobkovitz, and
" Wolf. The victory, after God, muft be afcribed to the wife
" and valourous conduct of marfhal Daun.* Count Stambach, ge-
" neral of horfe, who commanded the left wing, contributed very
" much to the victory, by the vigorous attack he made on the
                                K   " enemy's

* Leopold count Daun was born in 1705. He was, in the beginning, a knight of Malta, and colonel of his father's regiment: in 1736 lord of the bed-chamber; in 1737 major general, and ferved againft the Turks; in 1739 a lieutenant general; in 1740 he obtained a regiment; in 1745 he was made a general of infantry; in 1748 a privy councillor; in 1751 commandant of Vienna; in 1753 knight of the golden fleece; and in 1754 a field marfhal.

" enemy's right. Lieutenant generals Kolowrat, Wolwart, Wied,
" and Sincere; major generals Schallenberg, Le Fevre, and Niclas
" Efterhafi, diftinguifhed themfelves very much: as did general
" Nadafti,* with the Saxon light horfe, and the other troops
" under his command. The regiments that formed the referve,
" and the grenadiers, fuffered very much; having been continu-
" ally in action. Among the infantry, the regiment of Botta,
" commanded by prince Kinfky, diftinguifhed itfelf; having fired
" all their cartridges, they however continued in the line, with
" their bayonnets fixed, and repulfed the enemy. Among the
" cavalry, the four regiments of Savoy, Ligne, Birkenfeld, and
" Wurtenberg, diftinguifhed themfelves in a particular manner.
" The artillery, commanded by colonel Feuerftein, was remarkably
" well ferved. Among the volunteers, the duke of Wurtenberg,
" and major general count Czernichew,† likewife diftinguifhed
" themfelves."

He had, in the preceding war, fhewn no lefs bravery than prudence; and was wounded in the battles of Grotzka and Freidberg, in 1749. He formed the new exercife, and compofed the inftitutions for the new military academy. In 1745, having quitted the order of Malta, he married the countefs Fuchs, (a favourite of the empreſs) by whom he has many children. He is a middle fized man, and has the moft engaging countenance that can be feen: is uncommonly brave, and cool in action: a degree more of that vigor animi, would make him one of the greateft men of his age.

* General Nadafti is a Hungarian born: he ferved at firft as lieutenant colonel in Baronial's regiment of huffars; and in 1736 colonel; in 1741 major general; in 1744 lieutenant general; in 1753 a privy councillor; in 1754 commandant of Buda, and general of horfe; in 1756 bann of Croatia; and in 1758 a field marfhal. He ferved in Italy, Silefia, and on the Rhine; and diftinguifhed himfelf greatly in the paffage of that river, in the preceding war; and by the taking of Schweidnitz in 1757. To recompence his fervices, her imperial majefty reftored him his grandfather's eftates; and, though a Hungarian, conferred upon him the government of Buda. He was married in 1745, and has feveral children. Some difguft happened between him and the other commanders, after the battle of Liffa, and he never appeared more in the army.

† Count Czernichew is a Ruffian born: he was firft an enfign in the Semonowfki life guards; and in 1756 a major general. He is a man of great parts, which have contributed to advance his fortune. At prefent he is fecretary of war.

THE

The Prussians account of this battle is as follows:

"Immediately after the battle of Prague, colonel Putkammer, with his huffars, was sent to purfue the enemy; who was followed, on the 9th of May, by the the prince of Bevern and general Zeithen,* with 20,000 men. The firft remarkable fkirmifh happened at Suchdol, where the Auftrians great magazine of meal was taken. Lieutenant general Ziethen, and major generals Krochow and Manftein, with four battalions, and 1100 horfe, were fent from the camp at Kollin on this expedition. They fucceeded in taking this magazine, notwithftanding there was a camp of huffars and Croats behind Suchdol, and the heights by St. John's chapel was occupied by the Auftrians. General Nadafti fent lieutenant colonel Ballafti, with fome hundred huffars, to attack lieutenant colonel Varnery, of Putkammer's regiment, but they were repulfed with lofs. Colonel Werner, being fent to obferve the Auftrians, was attacked, near Krattenau, by colonels Zobel and Lufinfki, with 600 horfe, which he repulfed, and took 43 prifoners. On the 5th of June, the prince of Bevern quitted his camp at Kollin, in order to attack general Nadafti's corps, who was encamped on the heights near St. John's chapel; but this general made no ftand, either there, or on the heights by Kank; which he quitted, as well as the town of Kuttenberg. We took 73 prifoners: and the enemy loft, killed and wounded, above 150 men

---

* This general is greatly favoured by the king. In 1740 he ferved as major of huffars, in Silefia; in 1741 was lieutenant colonel, and decorated with the order pour le merite; and in the fame year a colonel, and had a regiment given him; in 1744 a major general; in 1756 a lieutenant general. After the battle of Prague, in which he diftinguifhed himfelf, he was made knight of the black eagle. He has commonly commanded the vanguard. After the battle of Breflaw, he made a fine retreat. In the battle of Torgau he gained immortal glory, by occupying the heights of Süptitz, fter the king had been forced to quit the field, which tore the victory out of M. Daun's hands. He is now above 60 years old.

" men more. The prince of Bevern, on this occasion, took two
" magazines of forage and provisions, at Kuttenberg and Neuhoff,
" and encamped by Neschkarziz, a village between Neuhoff and
" Kuttenberg. This position forced M. Daun to quit his strong
" camp at Czaslaw, and fall back first to Goltzjenkau, and after-
" wards to Haber. The great number of defiles hindered us
" from attacking the enemy's rear-guard, so that this march was
" made without any skirmish, excepting that which happened on
" the 7th of June, at the defile of Czûrckwitz, which alarmed
" general Nadasti, who was encamped behind Czaslaw, with his
" corps reinforced by the four regiments of Saxon horse. In the
" mean while, the army under M. Daun, having been reinforced,
" amounted to 60,000 men; and it appeared, his intentions were
" to march, with the greatest part of his troops, against that part
" of the king's camp, before Prague, on the other side of the
" Moldau; and, to cover this manœuvre, to attack the prince of
" Bevern with Nadasti's corps. The prince of Bevern had only
" 70 squadrons and 18 battalions, and consequently was in need of
" a reinforcement. The king, therefore, having drawn his posts
" before Prague nearer together, broke up the 13th of June, and
" marched with 10 battalions and 20 squadrons, by Kosteletz, to-
" wards Zasinuck. On the same day, count Daun ordered gene-
" ral Nadasti to attack prince Bevern's fore-posts, and at the same
" time made a motion with his whole army on the Prussians flank,
" which forced them to retire towards Kollin, and on the 14th
" to Kaurzim, where the king's corps joined them. The 15th
" and 16th were employed in reconnoitring the roads towards the
" village of Wisocka, where the Austrian army stood; which was
" not perfectly executed on account of the great number of the
" enemy's light troops. Four thousand pandours and hussars
" attacked a transport coming from Nimburg, but the escort,
" consisting

" confifting of 200 men, under major Billerbeck, defended them-
" felves above three hours; and, having received a reinforcement,
" arrived fafe at the camp with the lofs of feven men only. On
" the 17th, as we propofed marching to Schwoyfitz, we perceived
" the enemy's army formed on the heights, in a half fquare,
" with the right wing extending towards Kuttenberg and Kollin,
" and the left towards Zafmuck; the front was covered by a
" chain of fifhponds and morafles. We made a motion, fo that
" our right came to Kaurzim, and our left towards Nimburg
" and Planian, before it. On the 18th we occupied fome hills
" before this place. The army marched on the left, in order to
" attack the enemy as foon as the neceffary difpofitions could be
" made; and our light troops had pofted themfelves oppofite thofe
" of the enemy, who endeavoured to form on our left flank; we
" drove them back beyond Kollin, as far as the heights, which
" we muft neceffarily occupy to be able to attack the enemy's
" right flank. Major general Hulfen,* with feven battalions,
" was ordered to render himfelf mafter of them. The infantry
" was to form a line to fuftain this attack, without engaging its
" right, which was ordered to remain fomewhat further back.
" Our grenadiers climbed up the heights, occupied a village the
" enemy had abandoned, and took two batteries, each of 12 or
" 13 pieces behind it; and, of a fudden, our infantry, without
" giving time to ftop them, advanced and attacked all the enemy's
" firft line, which hindered us from fuftaining the attack of the
" heights: four battalions would have fufficed, and the victory
" was ours. The enemy, taking advantage of this fault, ordered
                                                              " fome

* This general was major in 1740; in 1743 lieutenant colonel; in 1745 colonel; in 1754 major general, and knight of the order pour le merite; in 1756 he had a regiment; and in 1758 was made a lieutenant general. He commanded a confiderable corps in Saxony, againft the army of the empire, with much reputation, particularly in the action by Strehlen.

" some infantry to file behind the line, and attack our seven
" battalions; who, though they had suffered very much in three
" succeffive attacks, and from the fire of 40 pieces of cannon,
" repulsed them. Norman's dragoons attacked the enemy's in-
" fantry, disperfed several battalions, took 5 pair of colours, and
" then advanced againft the Saxon carabineers, whom they beat
" back and pursued as far as Kollin. While our infantry was
" engaged with the enemy, it suffered greatly from the heavy
" artillery: the battalions were full of large openings. The regi-
" ment of cavalry of the prince of Pruffia took poft oppofite the
" interval between the regiments of prince Bevern and prince
" Henry, in order to cover the abovementioned openings, and
" attacked an Auftrian regiment of foot that stood over againft
" them, and no doubt had penetrated, if it had not been expofed,
" at the fame time, to a battery charged with cartouches, which
" threw them back on Bevern's regiment. The Auftrian cavalry
" pursued them; whereby prince Bevern's and prince Henry's
" regiments suffered so much, that they were obliged to be
" ordered out of the line. This produced an opening that cut
" off our communication with the attack of the heights, and we
" were forced to retire. The battalion of guards, on the right,
" repulfed four battalions, and two regiments of horfe, who at-
" tempted to furround them. Our left wing remained on the
" ground, where the enemy was pofted before the action, 'till
" about 9 o'clock, and then retired. The army marched towards
" Nimburg without being followed at all. Several cannon have
" been left behind, the carriages being broke, and for want of
" horfes. The lofs of this battle obliges us to raife the fiege of
" Prague. The army on the right of the Moldau marched to-
" wards Brandeifs, and joined that which came from Kollin; and
" M. Keith, with his, marched to Budyn.

" The

" THE Prussians account of their loss, is 1450 men, and 1667
" horses, killed, in the cavalry; 8755 men, killed and missing,
" in the infantry; and 3568 wounded: in all, 13,773. The list,
" published at Vienna, of the loss of the Austrians, is 819 men
" killed, 3616 wounded, in the infantry; 163 men, 414 horses,
" killed, 825 men, and 748 horses, wounded, in the cavalry.
" Among the wounded were 23 staff officers, and marshal Daun
" himself."

THOUGH the two preceding accounts, particularly the last, are very clear and explicit, I will add that sent to France, because it is impossible that so important an action should be too much explained and examined.

" MARSHAL Daun, having received orders, on the 11th of
" June, to march to the relief of Prague, with full power to act
" as he should think most advantageous for the empress's service,
" quitted his camp the next morning, and, after a difficult march
" of some days, arrived on the 15th at Gintitz. His excellency
" proposed marching, the day following, to Kaurzim, which was
" the most commodious road to Prague. The king of Prussia had
" joined the prince of Bevern, with a considerable reinforcement,
" the preceding evening; and, as he had a perfect knowledge
" of the country, he no doubt believed, that, by occupying the
" camp of Kaurzim, he would very much embarrass marshal Daun.
" Effectively, when the marshal was informed of it, he perceived
" very well the great inconveniency in which the king had put him
" by taking this position, while it reduced him to the necessity of
" marching on his right, or on his left. It was extreamly dan-
" gerous and difficult to march on the left, on account of the
" defiles, morasses, and woods; and, if he marched on his right
" he must necessarily pass near Kaurzim, and present his flan
" to the enemy: and lastly, if, to avoid this, he would mar

"a great way about towards the right, he would be the next day
"farther from Prague than at present; and moreover would, by
"that means, afford the enemy an opportunity to take twenty
"other positions, equally proper to hinder him from approaching
"that place; which is very easy in this country, where advan-
"tageous camps can be found on every spot. The marshal, seeing
"therefore that he must necessarily come to an action, in order
"to deliver Prague, resolved to encamp the next morning in the
"enemy's presence, and reduce him to the necessity either of
"attacking, or give a proper opportunity of being attacked.
"Accordingly the army marched to Krichenau. On the 17th,
"the marshal, being informed that the enemy marched towards
"Planian, mounted instantly, and went to reconnoitre their mo-
"tions, in person. Perceiving that the king directed his march
"towards the Austrians right, he thought it necessary to change
"the position of his army. It was formed with Planian before
"the front: the left wing was placed, in two lines of infantry,
"with a great quantity of artillery, on a high hill, that stood
"quite alone, in the plain. On the right was another hill, some-
"what lower than the former; on this the rest of the infantry
"was posted, likewise in two lines, with two lines of cavalry
"on their flank. At the bottom of the hill, between these two
"heights, is a plain of about 2500 paces long; here the marshal
"put two lines of horse, and a third in reserve; because, as the
"king was equally strong in cavalry, it was imagined he would
"make his greatest efforts against the center, in order to cut the
"army in two. His excellency used all the possible precautions
"to elude the king's intention: artillery was placed on the flanks,
"and before the cavalry. Things continued in this situation the
"17th. On the 18th the king ordered his army to march on the
"left, along the great road that goes from Prague to Vienna, and

"he

" he endeavoured, continually, to come on the right flank of the
" imperial army. M. Daun, perceiving the king's intentions,
" ordered the corps de referve to march on the right wing, in
" order to cover the flank. Between 9 and 10 o'clock in the
" morning, the head of the king's army appeared near Slatifunz,
" about a mile and a half off, where he continued 'till midday,
" in order to give his columns time to affemble: then all was put
" again in motion, and always directed their march towards the
" Auftrians right flank. The marfhal, who expected this, ordered
" his fecond line to march there, and clofe up with the referve.
" At half an hour paft one, the head of the Pruffian columns,
" both infantry and cavalry, appeared oppofite the imperial army;
" which was prepared to receive them. The Pruffian infantry
" formed immediately, and advanced, in good order, to attack
" the marfhal; who likewife marched to meet them. About
" 2 o'clock, the attack, fupported by a numerous artillery, began
" with fuch incredible vivacity, that an eye witnefs only can form
" a proper idea of it. The imperial army anfwered with a con-
" tinual fire, both of fmall arms, and heavy artillery. The king
" of Pruffia had pofted fome heavy cannon on a hill, behind his
" infantry, which did the imperial army much damage. This
" firft attack lafted about an hour and a half; then the fire of the
" imperial army began to be fuperior to that of the Pruffians,
" and forced them to quit the field of battle, that they might
" reft, and put themfelves in order to renew the action. This
" was executed foon after; but they were repulfed, as in the firft.
" Seven fucceflive attacks were made from 2 o'clock 'till half an
" hour paft fix, when the laft and moft violent was made. This
" attack was general, and lafted 'till paft 7 o'clock, when the
" Pruffians were forced to give way on all fides, and retire in
" confufion. The marfhal fent fome infantry and cavalry to-

L   purfue

" purfue them. The corps of light troops, under general Nadafti,
" followed them a great way, and brought in many prifoners.
" The Saxon carabineers ftood over againft fome Pruffian infantry,
" from which, as well as from the artillery, they fuffered very
" much: they defired leave to attack them; which, having ob-
" tained, they executed it with much bravery, cut the enemy's
" infantry to pieces, and took feveral cannon and colours. This
" is what happened on the right wing, where the battle was
" hotteft. About two hours after the firft attack on our right,
" that of the Pruffian army advanced againft the left of the
" Auftrians, in order to attack it; which, confidering the ftrength
" of its pofition, ought never to have been undertaken. It ftood
" upon a hill which was almoft impoffible to afcend, and which
" was covered with artillery that did the Pruffians great damage.
" The Pruffians right wing, being arrived at the bottom of the
" hill, ftopped: upon which the Auftrians left, feeing the ene-
" my did not advance, being defirous to attack them, and par-
" take of the glory of the day with the reft of the army, quitted
" their pofition, and defcended to the foot of the hill. The
" Auftrian infantry attacked that of the Pruffians with much
" bravery; and, after an hour's combat, obliged them to give
" way. The Auftrian cavalry advanced likewife, in order to
" attack that of the enemy, but thefe immediately retired to-
" wards their infantry. The Auftrians were prudent enough not
" to purfue their advantages on this fide, for fear of being fepa-
" rated from their right wing. In about an hour after, the Pruf-
" fians right wing attacked the Auftrians left again; but, in lefs
" than half an hour, they were beat back in confufion. They
" refumed their former pofition, and fired from all their artillery
" upon the Auftrians, during the whole action. While the fecond
" attack was made, fix battalions, commanded by count Niclas
Efterhafi,

"Efterhafi, having fhot all their cartridges, advanced againft the
enemy with fixed bayonnets, and, with great bravery, forced
them to give way. This battle was general, and all the corps
were more than once engaged, &c."

As this remarkable action makes a confiderable epoch in the hiftory of the war, being the firft the king of Pruffia ever loft, we fhall here give our reflections upon it, and upon the different manœuvres that preceded it.

Reflections on the battle of Kollin.

It has been already obferved, that the fiege of Prague, with about 50,000 men in it, was an imprudent and dangerous enterprize. Sieges are attended with fo great expence, and fo much lofs of time, and men, that they ought never to be undertaken without the utmoft neceffity. The king of Pruffia was then in circumftances that required fome decifive ftroke; and that as foon as poffible; and therefore he fhould not, by any means, amufe himfelf with fieges, which he knew would give the Auftrians time and means to provide for their defence, whatever was the event of that of Prague. Sieges muft never be formed, unlefs, 1. when the fortreffes are placed on the paffes which lead into the enemy's country, and in fuch a manner that you cannot penetrate 'till you are mafters of them; 2. when they are on your communications, and the country does not furnifh the neceffary fubfiftence; 3. when they are neceffary, in order to cover the magazines you form in the country itfelf, to facilitate your operations; 4. when they contain confiderable magazines of the enemy, and fuch as are effentially neceffary to him; 5. when the conqueft of them is necessarily followed by that of fome confiderable diftrict, which enables you to feparate your armies into winter quarters in the enemy's

country.

country. In these cases, your first operation must, no doubt, be the siege of some such place; which in all others must be avoided. Not one of these circumstances concurred with regard to Prague: it covers no essential pass into the country, neither contained any considerable magazine, nor was necessary for the king in order to form one there, because the country itself furnished abundantly all kind of subsistence; and, though it did not, his armies could be supplied from Silesia, without any risk; for prince Charles could not, if he remained at or about Prague, prevent it. If, instead of besieging this town, his majesty had sent 20,000 men, the next morning, after the enemy's right wing, which, as we have said, had fled to Beneschau, and, with the remainder, marched to Böhmisch Brodt against M. Daun, it is more than probable he would have destroyed both: they certainly could not have retired without losing their artillery, baggage, &c. and must have fell back, with the utmost expedition, on the Danube. Then the king was at liberty to besiege Olmutz; which would have given him all Bohemia; because prince Charles must likewise have marched on the Danube, in order to join the remainder of the army, as he could not, in the situation in which he then was, without any magazines or artillery, undertake any thing himself: he could not even approach the king at all, without exposing his army to destruction. His majesty might have taken twenty positions that would have covered the siege of Olmutz, masked the Danube and the capital, and forced prince Charles to march up to Lintz, in order to pass it, and join the rest of the troops. This would have given him all the time necessary to reduce Olmutz, and even Prague itself, which would have been left to a common garrison. His majesty, allured by the uncertain and vain, but flattering, hopes of taking 50,000 men prisoners, lost sight of Daun and the right wing, and with it an opportunity of giving some decisive blow. When he

was

was informed of the enemy's approach, it was still time to repair the fault he had committed. He might, and ought to have raised the siege of Prague, and, with his whole forces, attack M. Daun; if he succeeded, it was very probable that prince Charles, in so long a march as he must make from Prague to the Danube, would give an opportunity to attack him also; and he could scarce approach the Danube at all, while the king was with an army near Kollin, as is evident from the inspection of the map.

His majesty knew that prince Bevern narrowly escaped being oppressed by the superior forces of the enemy; How could he think that the addition of a few battalions and squadrons would insure the victory? His whole army was scarce sufficient to contend with Daun, and yet he persists in his first project of taking Prague, and thereby exposed himself to certain destruction, if the enemy had done part only of what might have been easily executed, as well by the garrison of Prague, as by M. Daun after the battle. It is one of the most essential qualities of a general, not to be infatuated with a passion for some favourite and striking project, because it exposes him to many, and sometimes fatal, consequences. It is difficult to renounce to an enterprize once embraced, because it in some measure exposes one to the censure of want of foresight, or constancy, both very mortifying to self-love. However, there is more glory in mending a fault, than to persevere in it. His majesty, confiding too much in his own superior talents, too little in those of his enemies, or pressed, perhaps, by the necessity of his affairs, has been observed, very often, to undertake things much above the means he had to accomplish them; and therefore no wonder that many of his projects, though in appearance plausible, wanted solidity, and consequently have not been always attended with success. Being arrived at Kaurzim, and finding the enemy too strongly posted to be attacked with any probability of success,

his

his majesty might have fell back, and taken some other position, which perhaps would have induced them to advance, and give him an opportunity to fight upon more equal terms: if it be objected that prince Charles, informed of his absence, would attack the army left before Prague, it only proves he was sensible he had exposed that army to destruction, as it depended on the enemy's knowing a thing, which he might have done by a thousand means. When he resolved to occupy the heights on the right flank of the enemy, he ought not surely to have marched at broad day, because they must necessarily perceive his intention, and in time to make their dispositions accordingly, as it happened. Possibly if the king had sent in the evening a great corps of cavalry, which he could spare in that mountainous country, towards the enemy's left flank, it would have drawn their attention that way, and given him an opportunity to march unobserved in the night, and occupy the height of Chotzemitz: the attempting it by day made it impossible from the first instant. His majesty in marching formed a portion of a circle; the enemy marched on the Chord, and therefore could with ease bring more men into action, at any one point of attack, and in less time, than he could do, though the armies had been equal, which must be decisive; as his majesty was in proportion much stronger in cavalry than in infantry, he ought no doubt to have chosen the most convenient ground on the enemy's front for that species of troops; and, as he had given them an opportunity to reinforce their right, and its flank, where they had brought two thirds of their army, he ought to have refused both his wings, and make an effort with his cavalry, sustained by infantry and artillery, on the center, between Chotzemitz and Brzist, where the enemy had only cavalry; and therefore most probably would have been forced to give way, and their two wings, being thus separated, easily defeated; whereas, by persisting to attack their right, he could

bring

bring only his infantry to action, the ground being very improper for cavalry, as well on account of the ravins and woods, as of the villages before the enemy's front. Having resolved to attack this wing, his majesty should have brought here all his infantry, leaving only a line of horse on his right, which would have been sufficient, as the enemy's left could never quit their advantageous position and descend into the plain. This would have enabled him to sustain his vanguard properly, and at a convenient distance; whereas he left it exposed, and quite in the air, his line being too far back: the more successful his vanguard was, the more certain to be destroyed, because the more they advanced, the more they exposed themselves to be attacked on all sides, as it really happened: for, having pierced the first line of the enemy, and attacked the flank of the second, they found themselves engaged with the greatest part of the army in front; and the whole reserve, composed of infantry and cavalry, on their flank; and at the same time exposed to the fire of a very numerous and well served artillery: and, being so far advanced that they could not be sustained by the line, were obliged to give way. If they had been properly supported, and a body of troops sent on their flank, opposite the enemy's reserve, to keep it in awe, the battle was won: the enemy's line was already broke, and had no convenient ground behind to take a new position upon; so that the whole army would have been taken in flank; nor could the reserve quit its position to attack this vanguard in flank, without presenting their own, and losing the advantage of their situation. But, as these dispositions were not made, the enemy's reserve, without any risk, quitted its post, and took the king's vanguard in flank, which, as has been said, being unsupported by any other troops, was forced to give way, and the battle was lost. The general faults therefore of the king's disposition, before, and during the action, were, 1. to have

manœuvred

manœuvred by day, which gave the enemy time to change their position, according to their circumstances; 2. to have formed an attack where he could not conveniently combine the different species of arms; whereas the enemy had both infantry and cavalry, with a great quantity of artillery, to sustain the point attacked; 3. to have let general Hulsen advance so far, that he could not be supported by the line; and, 4. to have attacked with too little infantry, considering the nature of the ground.

As to the conduct of M. Daun, it appears uniform, and founded upon reasonable principles: after the battle of Prague, it was very judicious; he retired before the duke of Bevern, though stronger than him from the beginning, as well to give his men time to recollect themselves, as to be able to receive the reinforcements he expected. These being arrived, his conduct changes according to the circumstances; he is now as vigorous and active, as he seemed before slow and dilatory. His march was calculated to cut off the prince of Bevern, before he could join the army at Prague, or be reinforced by it; and, though this project did not succeed, it was certainly well laid. His conduct, during the action, appears no less prudent. The enemy made no fault of which he did not take advantage: one only he himself seems to have committed, which was to have kept his line too far back: this gave Hulsen an opportunity of taking the villages, before the front, from between them and the front, and then penetrate through the line, which would certainly have occasioned the loss of the battle, had he been properly supported. Whenever your line is placed behind villages, it must be at a proper distance to sustain them, otherwise they, being taken, will be of great prejudice to you, and advantage to the enemy, whose motions are covered and sustained by them; whereas, if you sustain them properly, he cannot possibly take them, nor advance, leaving them behind; because not only they

break

break his line and throw it into some degree of confusion, which favourable opportunity, if improved, will necessarily be attended with a defeat, and also expose it to be taken in flank by the troops posted in them. The possession therefore of villages, provided they are at a proper distance to be sustained, is one of the most advantageous circumstances that can occur in a field of battle; but all these advantages are lost, and turn against you, if you do not sustain them. They are so very advantageous that I would never advise any general to attack them, if he sees they will be sustained, but rather mask them, and put them on fire with haubitz, and choose some other point of attack, which, though in appearance less proper, will, generally speaking, succeed better.* If the marshal had marched the 19th with his whole army towards Prague, it is probable that of the king, before that place, would have been destroyed. In war a general must think he has done nothing, while something remains unfinished; he ought to consider all his successes as means only that lead to greater, but never make an epoch of them, or pause to meditate, while in the full career of victory and glory.

On the 19th his majesty quitted the army, which had fought at Kollin, and went to Prague, in order to raise the siege: this was executed the day following without any loss worth mentioning; that part of the army which was on the right of the Moldau, marched down that side as far as Leutmeritz, while

---

* We have a fine example of this given by the famous Marlborough, at the battle of Hockstedt; he had attacked several times the village of Oberklaw, but was each time repulsed with great loss; his lordship, very judiciously having left a body of infantry to mask the village, advanced, and broke the enemy's line, which got the battle. The French had garnished all the villages before their front, particularly Oberklaw and Plentheim, with a prodigious quantity of infantry, expecting that the generals of the allies would attack them, and by no means presume to advance and leave them behind; but they were disappointed, beat, and lost all their infantry posted in the villages.

while that under M. Keith took the road of Welwarn and Budyn, where he paſſed the Egra, and went to encamp between Libofchowitz and Lowoſitz, oppoſite the king's diviſion; ſo that the whole formed only one army, ſeparated by the Elbe, over which they had the neceſſary communications, and could eaſily be on either ſide, according as circumſtances might require. With the remainder of his forces his majeſty had formed another conſiderable army, amounting to above 30,000 men, under the command of the prince of Pruſſia, who took poſt about Böhmiſch Leipa. By this means it was thought they could effectually cover Saxony and Luſatia, and keep open the communication through this laſt province with Sileſia: for, if the enemy marched down the left of the Elbe, and attempted to penetrate into Saxony, by the way of Auſſig, the king could, with his army encamped about Leutmeritz, paſs the river, and take ſuch poſitions between Lowoſitz and Auſſig, as would effectually put a ſtop to their progreſs; and, if they directed their ſteps towards Luſatia, the prince's army could eaſily take ſome advantageous camp in that mountainous country, which would enable him, though inferior, to oppoſe them with ſucceſs, at leaſt till the king had time to make ſome manœuvre in his favour.

While his majeſty was thus occupied in making diſpoſitions to continue in Bohemia as long as poſſible, the Auſtrians were no leſs active in forming their plan to drive him out of it. This could be accompliſhed in three different ways: the firſt was to follow M. Keith down the left of the Elbe, and endeavour to penetrate into Saxony, the conqueſt of which would open the way to carry the war into Brandeburg, and probably furniſh ſome opportunity to put a happy end to it; and the more ſo, as the Ruſſians and Swedes would be at hand to act in concert, and conſequently with more vigour: the ſecond method propoſed, was to

leave

leave an army to obferve the enemy, and to fend the remainder into Silefia, either to befiege Neifs or Schweidnitz, which, it was imagined, would force the enemy to quit Bohemia, in order to cover thefe important places, on which the prefervation of Silefia feems very much to depend: the third and laft method that offered, was to keep the army together, and march towards Lufatia, which would force the enemy to retire, or come to an action: and, as this laft was moft probable, from the known character of the king, it would be advifeable to have the whole army united, rather than feparate it, to undertake many things at once, and fo expofe it to be beat in detail. This plan was preferred to the others: accordingly, the whole Auftrian army paffed the Elbe on the 1ft of July, and encamped at Liffau, which the enemy had quitted the 26th of laft month, and marched fucceffively to Jungbuntzlaw and Tfcheditz, on the right of the Ifer.

PRINCE Charles fent general Nadafti, with a confiderable corps, likewife on the right of that river, as well to obferve the enemy's motions at Leutmeritz, as to cover the march of the army towards Jungbuntzlaw. General Morocz was fent alfo, with a ftrong body, on the left of the Ifer, to obferve the prince of Pruffia's motions, and to prepare every thing for the march of the main army. The firft of thefe corps having taken poft at Mfchno, between the prince's army and that of the king, while the other paffed the Ifer at Bakehofen, on the prince's left flank, his royal highnefs thought it full time to quit Tfcheditz; and, as thefe two corps were continually on his flanks, he found it neceffary to fall back fucceffively to Hirfchberg, Neufchlofs, and Leipa; from whence he fent general Putkammer, with four battalions and 500 huffars, to occupy Gabel, that he might fecure that important pafs which leads into Lufatia.

In the mean time the Auſtrians grand army advanced with ſlow, but cautious and ſure ſteps, to Munchengratz, and from thence to Hunnerwaſſer. The enemy's poſition at Leipa, covered with the Poltz, was thought too ſtrong to be attacked; it was therefore reſolved to turn his left flank and attack Gabel, which would neceſſarily force him to retire, and at the ſame time open a ſure way into Luſatia. Accordingly, general Macquire, with a conſiderable detachment, ſuſtained by the vanguard, was ſent on this expedition. The army advanced to Nimes, in order to cover it. The place was taken the 15th, after a defence of thirty-ſix hours, and the army immediately paſſed the Poltz. All theſe manœuvres forced the prince of Pruſſia to quit Leipa; and having, with Gabel, loſt the neareſt communication with Zittau, where he had a ſtrong garriſon, and a very conſiderable magazine of every kind, he was obliged to make ſeveral forced and difficult marches by Kamentz, Georgenthal, Kreywitz, Rumburg, and Unterhennerſdorff, in order, if poſſible, to anticipate the enemy; but he was diſappointed; for, on the taking of Gabel, they had directed their march to Zittau, where they arrived the 19th, and were then bombarding the town with the moſt unrelenting fury. They had however neglected to inveſt it entirely; the prince ſeized this favourable opportunity, approached the place with his army, and having, during the preceding night, withdrawn the greateſt part of the ſtores, baggage, &c. on the 23d he retired, by Lôbau, towards Bautzen, without any other loſs than that of colonel Diereck, and about 200 men, who ſtill endeavoured to defend themſelves in that general conflagration, which conſumed one of the moſt populous and rich cities of Germany.

The Auſtrians having thus drove a conſiderable part of the enemy's forces out of Bohemia, and ſecured their communications with that country, by occupying Zittau and Gabel, they

reſolved

resolved to advance farther into Lusatia, and endeavour to cut off the enemy intirely from Silesia. Accordingly, the grand army marched the 25th from Zittau to Eckartsberg; from whence several detachments were sent on the left, to observe the motions of the enemy; and on the right, down the Neiss, in order to secure the passes into Silesia. A small corps of light troops, commanded by colonel Janus, had already penetrated into that country by the way of Trautenau; but it was too inconsiderable to undertake any thing of consequence.

His royal highness prince Charles resolved to continue in the neighbourhood of Zittau until the enemy quitted the frontiers and fell back into Saxony; which he knew they would soon be forced to do, in order to oppose the combined army, that was then forming in the empire, and preparing to march towards the Saala and Leipsig. While these things passed between prince Charles and the prince of Prussia, the king, with near 40,000 men, remained at Leutmeritz in great tranquility, as if he had been no ways concerned in the event. At length, however, the taking of Zittau roused him from his lethargy, and shewed him the unfavourable situation of his affairs, which nothing but superior conduct and activity could reinstate. On entering Bohemia, at the beginning of the campaign, Silesia had been left without any troops, excepting some weak garrisons to cover it. The enemy had taken such a position as made it difficult to send any succours there: they could, therefore, enter that country, and perhaps take some place of consequence before it could possibly be relieved.

To remedy these evils, his majesty quitted Leutmeritz the 20th, and marched successively to Pirna, where he passed the Elbe, Bischofffwerda, and Bautzen, where he arrived the 29th, and joined the army commanded by the prince of Prussia, who retired, and never appeared more in the field, and died soon after.

From hence his majesty marched to Weissenberg, and there waited 'till the arrival of marshal Keith; who, having left a small corps to protect Saxony, followed with the remainder, and joined him in the beginning of August. Having thus assembled a very considerable army, he resolved to open the communication with Silesia; and, if possible, bring the enemy to an action; which might, if successful, retrieve his affairs.

With these views, his majesty quitted Weissenberg on the 15th, and marched to Ostritz. His vanguard took general Beck's baggage at Bernstadtel; and some of the light troops, pushing on to Ostritz, they there surprized general Nadasti, at table; who, with the utmost difficulty, found means to escape. All his equipage was taken: some letters were found in it that indicated a design to betray Dresden to the Austrians. This served as a pretext to treat the queen of Poland with some hardship. On the 16th he advanced within cannon shot of the enemy, in order to give them battle; but he found them so advantageously posted, that he did not think it prudent to attack them. However, he continued here 'till the 20th; and then, finding they would not quit their position, returned to his former camp behind Ostritz. Though his majesty had not been able to execute his plan intirely, he had gained an important point by opening a communication with Silesia; which he resolved to keep so, if possible, that his forces might act in concert, at least, if not united. He left, therefore, in this neighbourhood, a considerable part of his army, under the command of the prince of Bevern; and, with the remainder, returned to Dresden, in order to march against the combined army, which was advancing towards Saxony.

Before we proceed to give an account of the ulterior operations of the respective armies, we think it may be useful to examine those which happened after the siege of Prague. In the description we have

have given of this country, it appears, there are three roads that go out of it into Lufatia: the firft, near the Elbe, goes by Leipa, Kamentz, and Rumburg, towards Bautzen; the fecond, along the Ifer, by Munchengratz, and Gabel, towards Zittau; the third, by Reichenberg, and Friedland, towards Lauban: all which are intercepted by many and great defiles, efpecially the firft and laft, where a corps, compofed of a few battalions, would fuffice to ftop an army. The plan, formed by the Auftrians, to act on the right of the Elbe, preferable to the left, was certainly well advifed; becaufe they could, with greater facility, drive the enemy out of Bohemia, than if they attempted it on the other fide, where he could take many pofitions between Lowofitz and Pirna, from whence they could not force him by any direct motion; and, if they endeavoured to get on his flanks, it would be attended with lofs of time, and perhaps would fail in the execution. This plan was attended with another great advantage, that, in forcing the enemy to retire out of Bohemia, by gaining his left flank, they cut him off from Silefia, and opened a fure way into it for themfelves.

As foon as the army pafied the Elbe, a large corps, under Nadafti, was fent to obferve the king; and another between that and the prince of Pruffia's army. Thefe two corps were fo ftrong, that when united they formed a fmall army, and could with fafety keep clofe to the enemy, and render the communication between their two armies very precarious. A third was fent on the prince's left flank; and, within a march of thefe different corps, the main army advanced under prince Charles. By this admirable difpofition he could fuftain them, if neceffary; and they had a fure retreat by falling back on his army: he was covered by them; and, keeping on the left of the Ifer, could not be forced to fight againft his will. His meafures were fo well taken, and executed with fo much

vigour

vigour and prudence, that in 20 days he forced the enemy to abandon Bohemia with great lofs, and cut off his communication with Silefia.

If, after the taking of Zittau, his royal highnefs had marched to Stromberg, beyond Lôbau, or to Reichenbach, or, laftly, to Jauernick, with a ftrong corps on the Landfcron, and the light troops in the woods behind Lôbau, the enemy could never have opened a communication with Silefia. The pofition of Kleinfchónau was too far back, and left the road between Bautzen and Górlitz open; fo that the king could always enter Silefia without any oppofition. The method, purfued by prince Charles, of acting with ftrong corps, rather than with the whole army, is attended with infinite advantages : 1. it facilitates the means of fubfifting, which, in every country, is difficult, when the army is very numerous; 2. it enables you to engage every day fome important combat, without bringing affairs to a decifion ; 3. they revive the fpirits of the foldiers, whom former misfortunes have rendered timid ; 4. by taking poft on the enemy's flanks you force him to quit every camp, however ftrong, and confequently to abandon the whole country. All which truths are deduced clearly from the conduct of prince Charles on this occafion.

That of the king does not, on the whole, appear in the fame favourable light. His activity in raifing the fiege of Prague is much to be commended; the leaft delay would have been fatal to him : his dividing the army into feveral ftrong corps, after the battle of Kollin, very much facilitated the retreat. Thefe prefented fo many objects to the enemy, that he could not immediately determine which was moft worthy his attention; nor could he undertake any thing againft them 'till he had afcertained their number, fpecies, and pofition : in the mean time they retired with tranquility and fafety. From the king's conduct, on this occafion, may be deduced a general rule for retreating after an action lost. That an army retreating must be divided into as many strong corps as the nature of the country will admit of; because, in this case, the enemy can do you no very essential damage: if he separates his army likewise into many corps, neither of them will be strong enough to undertake any thing of consequence; even, if they keep too close, they may receive some considerable check. Another advantage, arising from this method of retiring, is, that the enemy cannot intercept any one of your corps; because he can neither push between them, nor go so far about as to come before them, without exposing his own troops to be hemmed in between your different corps. If he follows you with his whole army, one only division can be in danger, which may be easily avoided by forming a strong rear-guard, who will get time for the remainder to march off in safety; and the more so, as a small corps marches much more lightly than an army. Care must be taken not to engage the whole corps; because, if the enemy is near, and acts with vigour, it will be lost intirely.

When prince Charles passed the Elbe, it was evident he proposed to advance towards Lusatia, consequently the king should have left M. Keith, with a few battalions and squadrons, in the mountains between Lowositz and Pirna, to cover Saxony, against the enemy's light troops, and with the remainder have taken a position behind the Poltz, about Leipa or Nimes, with a strong corps on his left, towards Liebenau, and another smaller on his right, between him and the Elbe, on the road to Rumburg. This would have made it impossible for the enemy to advance one step 'till they had dislodged him: they could not think of entering those great defiles, through which the road leading to Rumburg passes, having a corps, as I suppose, in front, and the whole army on their flank and rear; nor could they enter those of Liebenau and Reichenberg on his left, for the same reasons: they must consequently either force him to retire, or stop short. It was still more improbable that they would separate their army and send a considerable part of it to make an efficacious diversion in Silesia. Such is the strength of this country, and so many good camps to be found in it, that, if the prince of Prussia, even with his army, had taken the road of Gabel and Zittau, instead of that of Rumburg, it is probable he might have stopped prince Charles, for some time at least. The enemy did not choose to venture between his right flank and the king's army, and they could not easily take a position on his left, that could force him to quit Gabel and Zittau, if he had taken his camp on the mountains between these two places, which he ought to have done, rather than take the road of Rumburg, by which he lost them both, and his communication with Silesia. When the enemy arrived at Hunnerwasser, Why did not the king march instantly from Gastorff, and come on their flank and rear, while the prince his brother attacked them in front? Nothing in the world could hinder them from acting in concert. This, however, and many other favourable opportunities, which the enemy gave him, were lost. His majesty continued, as we have said, all this while, near Leutmeritz, in perfect tranquility.

The prince's army was, no doubt, too weak to withstand the efforts of the enemy, who were more than double his number; yet we think he might have taken such camps as would have stopped them. When a general has the misfortune to command an army that is much inferior to that of the enemy, he must certainly retire before them, if they send very strong corps on his flanks, as well because his subsistence becomes precarious, as because they may, by a judicious use of these corps, attack him with united forces in front and rear, and intirely defeat him; particularly if the country has many defiles. A general, in such circumstances, has

but

but one way to extricate himself; which is, to attack, with his whole forces, whatever corps may be sent on his flank: if he succeeds, once or twice, the enemy will scarce attempt a third time. The prince, having neglected to do this, was, as we have said, forced to retire from camp to camp, and at length to abandon the whole country.

DURING these transactions in Bohemia, the army of the empire, consisting of 32 squadrons, 32 battalions, 23 companies of grenadiers, 2 regiments of hussars, and 52 pieces of cannon, commanded by the prince of Hildburghausen, assembled in the circle of Franconia, in the month of August. These were to be reinforced by 30,000 French, under the command of prince Soubise, who had been for some time on the Main. Accordingly, they united at Erfurth on the 21st of August, and assumed the title of the combined army; the object of which, was, to drive the Prussians out of Saxony. This, it was thought, could be executed without any considerable difficulty. The country was in some measure defenceless, there being nothing to guard it but some few weak garrisons, which, though united, could form but an inconsiderable corps, incapable of keeping the field against such superior forces; and, being thus separated, were still less capable of making any effectual resistance. The king, being wholly taken up in observing the Austrians, had not, as they imagined, either time or means to come and oppose their operations.

FOR these reasons, it was resolved to march down the Saala and begin the campaign with the siege of Leipsig, preferable to any other enterprize, because they would be at hand to receive all kind of succours from Richlieu's army, now intirely at liberty by the convention of Closterseven, and moreover could, in case of success, take their winter quarters in this part of Saxony, and the next campaign proceed to the intire conquest of it, and of Magdeburg and Brandeburg.

THE king knew perfectly well, that, if the progress of the combined army, and that of M. Richlieu, was not immediately stopped, they would soon be on the Elbe; the consequence of which must be fatal to him. Having, therefore, left an army of 40 battalions and 70 squadrons, under the prince of Bevern, to defend Silesia, he quitted Bernstadtel the 25th of August, and marched to Dresden, where he assembled an army, and proceeded without delay to the Saala. On the 12th of September he arrived at Erfurth, which the enemy abandoned on his approach, and retired to Eisenach. His majesty followed them, intending to give them battle, but he found them so advantageously posted, that he did not think it adviseable to attack them; and, seeing they declined coming to an action as much as possible, he resolved to fall back on the Saala, as well to make his army subsist with more ease, as to be at hand to sustain a detachment which he proposed sending under prince Ferdinand, to cover Halberstadt and the neighbouring country, against the incursions of the light troops, which infested them daily from Richlieu's army; and another, under prince Maurice, between the Moldau and the Elbe, to cover that part of Saxony and Brandeburg. Accordingly, he retired first to Buttelstadt, and from thence to Naumburg, where he arrived the 13th of October. This retreat encouraged the combined army to advance; they resumed their former position at Erfurth, where general St. Germain was posted, with a considerable detachment, to observe the king's motions, and cover the remainder of the army, who, not being able to support the cold, were put into quarters of cantonment.

PRINCE Charles, seeing the enemy's forces thus separated at an immense distance, and the road into Brandeburg quite open, resolved to send a considerable detachment to Berlin; and, to cover this expedition, another great corps, under general Marshal, was sent upon the Elster. His royal highness proposed, by this enterprize,

to

to raife the credit of his arms, which the taking of the enemy's capital could not fail to do; to make a diverfion in favour of the combined army, becaufe it was not doubted but the king would quit Saxony for fome time, and haften to the fuccour of his refidence; and laftly, to oblige the prince of Bevern to make fome confiderable detachment, which would facilitate the means to drive him out of his prefent advantageous pofition.

ACCORDINGLY, general Haddick, with about 4000 men, was fent to Berlin; which he took, and ranfomed, and then retired behind the Spree with fafety and honour.

PRINCE Maurice, who, as hath been faid, had been detached towards the Elbe, was on his march there when he was informed of the enemy's enterprize againft Berlin; he immediately paffed that river, and directed his march towards Berlin, in hopes ftill to anticipate the enemy, or at leaft intercept him in his retreat; but, on his arrival at Schwelinz, advice was brought that Haddick had been at Berlin, and, having ranfomed it, was retired into Lufatia.

THE king, having been informed of this enterprize againft his capital, and believing at firft that the enemy had concerted fome folid plan with the Swedes, who were likewife advancing that way, thought it neceffary to go and defeat their defigns in perfon. For which purpofe, having left about 6000 or 7000 men, under M. Keith, to guard the Saala, and obferve the combined army, he quitted Leipfig on the 16th of October, and on the 20th arrived at Annaberg, on the right of the Elbe, where he was informed of Haddick's retreat. Upon which he ordered prince Maurice to refume his pofition between the Elbe and the Moldau, and with part of the troops returned to Leipfig.

THE generals of the combined army, now reinforced by a very ftrong corps, commanded by the duke of Broglio, refolved to feize this favourable opportunity which the king's abfence afforded them,

and

and once more penetrate into Saxony: accordingly, they put their troops in motion, paſſed the Saala on the 25th, and on the 27th had their head quarters at Weiſſenfels. From hence count de Mailly was ſent to ſummon Leipſig, which M. Keith refuſed to ſurrender. Things were in this ſituation, when the king arrived with about 10,000 men; and, being joined by the corps under M. Keith, and prince Ferdinand, an army of 22,000 men was aſſembled, with which he reſolved to march againſt the enemy.

Though the combined army was much ſuperior to that of the king, it was thought prudent to decline coming to an action, with the Saala behind them; and probably they meant to concert ſome new plan with M. Richlieu, now intirely diſengaged. Accordingly, the whole army repaſſed that river on the 29th; 4 battalions, and 18 companies of grenadiers, were left to defend Weiſſenfels; and 14 battalions, with ſome cavalry, under the command of the duke of Broglio, were ſent to occupy Merſeburg; which ſhews they then propoſed defending the banks of the Saala.

The king quitted Leipſig on the 30th, and arrived the day following at Weiſſenfels, which he ordered to be attacked inſtantly; and, after ſome reſiſtance, took it ſword in hand. The enemy, having for the moſt part paſſed the river, put fire to the bridge, which intercepted ſome of them, who were made priſoners. Their army was divided into two parts: the one, commanded by the prince of Hildburgſhauſen, remained oppoſite to Weiſſenfels; and the other, under prince Soubiſe, approached Merſeburg, to ſuſtain M. Broglio, or cover his retreat, in caſe it ſhould be thought convenient to abandon that place.

His majeſty knew, that, while the enemy had ſuch conſiderable forces on the frontiers of Magdeburg and Saxony, he could not think of ſeparating his army, to put the troops in winter quarters when the ſeaſon required it, even ſuppoſing he could keep the whole

whole in that country: it was therefore refolved to give the combined army battle, and, if they declined it, drive them fo far back that they could not refume their operations, at leaft for this campaign. Accordingly, bridges were thrown over the Saala, at Weiffenfels, Merfeburg, and Halle, where the army paffed in three columns, and affembled, the 2d of November, near the village of Rofbach, as in A. A. The enemy, having abandoned the defign of defending the banks of the Saala, quitted Merfeburg, and united their whole forces in B. B. The king examined their pofition the 3d, and refolved to attack them the next morning. Accordingly, he advanced at the head of his cavalry, in order to occupy thofe pofts which fhould be found moft proper to cover the infantry, and at the fame time form his difpofitions for the attack. Being arrived in D. D. he perceived they had, in the preceding night, changed their pofition, and taken another in C. C. which appeared too ftrong to be attacked: upon which the army was ordered to march on the left, and encamp in E. E. with the left at Rofbach, the center at Schartau, and the right towards Bedra, with the cavalry in the third line.

THE commanders of the combined army attributed this retrograde motion of the king to fear. This, and the great force of their army, elated their courage in fuch a manner, that they refolved to attack him next morning, and fo finifh the campaign; the fatigues of which their troops feemed no longer able or willing to endure. The king's right and center were deemed too well pofted to be attacked with fuccefs, confequently they propofed attacking the left on the flank and rear; and at the fame time general St. Germain was ordered to take poft, with a confiderable corps, in N. N. as well to amufe the enemy, as to cover the march of the army: at 11 o'clock it was put in motion, in three columns; the vanguard was compofed of Auftrian and imperial cavalry, followed by the

the French and imperial infantry; the whole was closed by the French horse. Being arrived on the hill, opposite the enemy's left flank, they halted, and ordered the French horse to advance, and join the rest of the cavalry at the head.

About 1 o'clock the king was informed that they were in march on his left flank; but, not being able as yet to discover their intentions, he remained quiet for the present, and observed them. At 2 o'clock he perceived they had passed his flank, and continued marching towards Merseburg; upon which he ordered his cavalry and artillery to march on the left, behind the hills, and occupy that near Lunstadt and Reichertswerben, while the infantry followed in all haste.

The generals of the combined army, seeing the enemy quit their camp with an appearance of precipitation, thought they were retiring; which seemed the more probable, as they could not discover any thing of the march, being covered by the hills. Anxious lest the enemy escaped, and they lose the fruits of their fine dispositions, they advanced in great haste with their cavalry, followed, at a considerable distance, by their infantry, hoping to overtake the rear-guard, and, by attacking it with vigour, either destroy it, or force the enemy to a general action. Being arrived near Reichertswerben, some of the enemy's horse appeared on the heights behind the village; they continued, however, to advance, thinking they were only posted there to gain time, and cover the retreat. This illusion soon vanished; all the Prussian horse was then forming, under the protection of some heavy artillery, posted on the hill, which did great execution, and contributed essentially to the success of the battle. As soon as they were formed, his majesty ordered them to attack that of the enemy; this they executed with promptitude and vigour, broke them, and drove them back in confusion to the village of Bufendorff, where they attempted to

rally;

rally; but the Prussians renewed their attack, without giving them time to execute it, broke them again, and so effectually, that they quitted the field. In the mean time the generals of the combined army endeavoured to form their infantry; but the king, who had as yet six or eight battalions only come up, ordered them instantly to advance, and attack the enemy, while they were occupied in forming the line. This was immediately executed; and, being supported by the cavalry and artillery, they easily broke those few troops which had formed at the head of the columns, and drove them back in confusion.

PRINCE Soubise, however, did not give up the affair as lost; the reserve, consisting of five regiments of cavalry, was ordered to advance and sustain the infantry, in order to form the line, if possible. These were instantly attacked, broke, and drove off the field; upon which the infantry, unsupported by its own cavalry, taken in flank by that of the enemy, and moreover exposed to a heavy fire of the artillery and small arms, were unable to keep their ground, much less form a line forwards: they attempted once more to form it behind, between the village of Busendorff and the Luftschiff, under the protection of some French cavalry; but these being over-powered, and forced to retire, after a vigorous combat, the infantry was likewise obliged to quit the field with precipitation. Count St. Germain covered the retreat.

THUS ended the battle of Rosbach; where 22,000 men, conducted with prudence and vigour, defeated above 50,000, with the inconsiderable loss of about 300 men, killed and wounded; whereas that of the combined army amounted to about 800 killed, and 6000 prisoners, including 11 generals and 300 officers, together with 72 pieces of cannon, and other military trophies. Many relations of this battle were published by authority: that of Vienna is too general, and gives a very imperfect idea of it; we shall, therefore, omit it, and give that of Berlin, and another wrote by an

officer

officer in the combined army; which, with what we have said on the subject, will enable the reader to form a proper judgment of this extraordinary transaction.

The Prussians account of the battle is as follows:

" In the beginning of September, the army of the empire, and
" the corps commanded by prince Soubise, assembled at Erfurth,
" intending to penetrate into Saxony, and render themselves masters
" of the Elbe: upon which part of the Prussian army marched
" towards Naumburg. Our light troops had a skirmish with those
" of the enemy, over which they gained a considerable advantage.
" The army passed the Saala, and advanced as far as Buttelstedt..
" About this time the convention of Bremerforde, between the:
" French and Hanoverians, was made, and a strong corps from the
" duke of Richlieu's army entered the principality of Halberstadt:.
" prince Ferdinand of Brunswic was sent there; he soon delivered:
" the country from the French, of whom he took 20 officers and
" 400 men; but, as the duke of Richlieu advanced with his whole
" army, prince Ferdinand retired to Wansleben, from whence he
" could intercept their convoys. His majesty's army marched to
" Erfurth, which the enemy quitted and retired into the moun-
" tains behind Eisenach. We had a post at Gotha; prince Hild-
" burghausen attacked it, but was repulsed with loss. Both armies
" continued in this situation 'till the end of October, when a corps
" of Hungarian troops marched through Lusatia into Brandeburg:
" it was thought that general Marshal's corps would follow them,
" which obliged his majesty to send prince Maurice to oppose
" them, and he himself followed, and advanced as far as Annaberg,
" to intercept them; but the enemy's expedition had no other ob-
" ject than to raise contribution, and, on the approach of prince
" Maurice, they retired without having collected it at all. While
" part of our army marched to succour the electorate, M. Keith,
" with

" with the reft, retired into Leipfig. The generals of the com-
" bined army believed this a favourable moment to put their pro-
" jects in execution: accordingly they marched cantonwife, part
" by Naumburg and Zeitz, and part by Weiffenfels, in order to
" take Leipfig, and our great magazine at Torgau. Our army
" was ordered to affemble at Leipfig, where the different corps
" arrived the 26th of October. On the 31ft we marched, intend-
" ing to attack the enemy's quarters; we made fome prifoners,
" but went no farther than Lutzen. His majefty, being informed
" that the enemy retired on all fides, marched with the vanguard
" to Weiffenfels. This city was defended by fome of the Bava-
" rian and Circle's troops: we attacked it, and took it, with about
" 300 prifoners: the enemy burnt the bridge over the Saala to
" facilitate their flight. The troops of the empire encamped on the
" other fide of the river, over againft Weiffenfels, pofted behind
" the enclofures and the houfes, in order to hinder us from re-
" pairing the bridge: they formed a chain on the left fide of the
" river; and marfhal Keith, who, with the greateft part of the
" army, was marched to Merfeburg, found the bridge burnt, and
" the town occupied by 14 French battalions, a detachment of
" which broke down the bridge at Halle. The field marfhal went
" with a detachment to this laft place, and ordered the bridge
" to be repaired, which obliged the enemy to abandon their pofts
" on the Saala, and retire towards Micheln. We repaired im-
" mediately the other bridges, and paffed the river by Merfeburg,
" Halle, and Weiffenfels: the three columns affembled on the fame
" day near the village of Rofbach. His majefty, having recon-
" noitred the enemy, found that they could be attacked on the
" right flank with advantage, which was refolved to be executed
" the following day: accordingly we marched, the cavalry having
" the vanguard. When we arrived on the heights, from whence

" the day before we had examined the enemy's position, we
" found they had changed it: their front was not only parallel
" to ours, but was covered by a deep ravin; their right was in a
" wood, on a high hill, covered also with three redoubts and an
" abbattis.* It was not thought prudent to attack them in this
" advantageous position, and so we returned to our old camp.
" The enemy, perceiving we did not attack them, ordered some
" detachments to follow us; they fired a few cannon shot at our
" cavalry, but without effect. The 5th, in the morning, we were
" informed the enemy were in motion on their right; and, soon
" after, that their whole army was in march: about noon we
" perceived the heads of their columns opposite to the flank of
" our left wing: we would take no resolution 'till we knew per-
" fectly their intentions. About 3 o'clock we perceived they
" had passed our left wing, and directed their march towards
" Merseburg: upon which our army was formed in order of battle,
" and, having made a motion on the left, we costed them: we
" reached the heights, which our cavalry occupied in such a man-
" ner, that they came on the flank of that of the enemy, and
" after several attacks broke and dispersed them. Our infantry
" reached the village of Reichertswerben, where our left was
" posted; and, as we perceived the French infantry form in co-
" lumns, in order to attack us, we anticipated them. The bat-
" tle lasted about an hour and a half: six battalions only of our
" left wing came to action. We followed the enemy to Burgwer-
" ben: the night hindered us from reaping still greater advantages
" from our victory. The day following our army marched to-
" wards Freidburg: the 7th a strong detachment passed the Saala,
" and advanced to Eckartsberg, &c. &c."

* Trees cut down, and placed so as to form a parapet; behind which the troops, particularly infantry, are placed.

THE

The next was wrote by a French officer in the combined army.

"It was refolved to attack the left flank of the Pruffian army: accordingly, at nine in the morning, our's marched in two columns. General St. Germain was ordered to take poſt before our camp, with 9 battalions and 14 or 15 ſquadrons, in order to attack the enemy in front, when he perceived that we did the ſame on his flank. The king, having been informed of theſe motions, which he ſo much deſired, left his camp ſtanding, with part of his army in it, to oppoſe St. Germain, and to make us believe he was in perfect ſecurity. The left wing of his army was hid behind a hill, and covered by ſome marſhy ground, and a village: part of his army was formed behind the above-mentioned hill, on which was a great quantity of artillery. Not far from this hill is another, which joins it, and extends far into the plain. Behind this hill the enemy had his infantry in columns, a great quantity of artillery, and almoſt his whole cavalry. Our army, having marched about two hours, was now oppoſite the enemy's flank; we had a fine plain before us, and, perceiving no enemy, we haſtened our march. It looked as if we feared the enemy ſhould eſcape us, and only reconnoitred his front, without taking any notice of his left wing; ſo were we heartily chaſtiſed for it. About half an hour after three our cavalry ſtruck in with that of the enemy, which ſtood at the bottom of the ſecond hill, and advanced in good order againſt ours, whom they could eaſily break; becauſe the cavalry of the empire was ſo cloſe to them, that they could not fire freely, nor could they form in good order. When the enemy firſt appeared, the cavalry of the left wing was ordered to advance, which they executed full gallop; but they found that of the right wing retiring in confuſion. Notwithſtanding
"this,

"this, the Austrian cavalry, and the regiments of Bourbon, La-
"meth, and Fitzjames in particular, fought with success. Scarce
"was the combat between the cavalry engaged, when the enemy
"directed his artillery to play on the front and flank of our ca-
"valry and infantry. Our infantry was immediately formed, but
"in some places they were too close, and in others had large open-
"ings; they moved to the left, where some brigades were soon
"repulsed by the fire of the Prussians: that of Mailly followed
"them; that of Wittmer, of which was the regiment of Dies-
"bach, kept its ground the longest; and prince Soubise was
"obliged to go himself and order it to retire."

ALL the other accounts concur in the principal circumstances, and therefore it seems needless to add any more.

REFLECTIONS.

THE generals of the combined army do not seem to have formed any fixed plan of operations, as if they proposed acting according to circumstances, as they occasionally arose: at first they seem willing to occupy Saxony, provided it might be done without any risk; they avoid coming to an action during the whole campaign, and at last, when it was least proper, they engage it. When the king quitted the Saala, having there only 12,000 men in two different corps, then was the time to advance and attack Leipsig; they might have taken many positions, which would have made it difficult, and perhaps impossible, for the king to relieve it; as he had no more than 10,000 men with him, and about 6000 men under prince Maurice; so that they would have had only these 16,000 men to contend with. As to the corps under prince Ferdinand, he might easily have been forced under the cannon of Magdeburg; any small detachment from the right of Richlieu's

army

army would have been sufficient for that purpose. Having suffered the king to unite his different corps at Leipsig, it was prudent, no doubt, to repass the Saala, because it is of too dangerous a consequence to engage an action with a great river behind the army; but they should have defended the banks of that river. As they were much stronger than the king, he could not pass it without their knowledge: if they left a strong detachment over against Weissenfels, and another at Merseburg, and with the army had taken a central position between these two places, they could, by an easy march, sustain either of them; and therefore, in all probability, have hindered the enemy from passing at all. If they proposed fighting, they could not have a better opportunity than while the enemy was passing the river; and, if they did not, they should have gone behind the Unstrut, and covered themselves with that river. It is agreed upon, by every one, that the king's army passed the Saala in three columns; one at Weissenfels, another at Merseburg, and the third at Halle; by which means they were separated from each other about seven miles; and that they united at Rosbach. We cannot conceive why the generals of the combined army permitted the enemy to commit so great a fault, without punishing him for it: they could have taken many positions to prevent the junction of these columns; and could, with their united forces, attack either of them separately; as appears evident, from the inspection of the map. Having, during the campaign, declined coming to an action, they should have persisted in that resolution a few days longer; because, from the situation of affairs in Silesia and in Westphalia, it was probable the king would be forced to go against the Austrians in person; and, though he did not, it was impossible for him to oppose effectually the combined army, and that of Richlieu, now disengaged, because he must necessarily have one or the other upon his flank; and, having about a fifth part of their forces only, he muft have abandoned the country, or fell a victim to fuperiority, if he perfifted to wait for them; fo that in this very campaign he would have loft either Saxony or Silefia, and perhaps both, had M. Richlieu and the generals of the combined army acted with more judgment.

The plan they formed to attack the enemy's left flank was inconfiftent with all the rules of military prudence; becaufe, in cafe of a defeat, there was no retreat at all for them: they had a river behind them, and the enemy between them and the country to which they muft necefiarily retire. The conduct of the action was no lefs imprudent; they could not think the enemy would permit them to invelope his left wing, and cut him off from the Saala; and, as they marched at mid-day, he could not be deceived as to their intentions. No general will fuffer an enemy to attack him in flank and rear: How could they imagine fuch a general as the king of Pruffia would commit this fault? When they refolved to attack his left flank, they fhould have made fome demonftrations on his right, to draw his attention that way: and, by marching in the night, approach his left flank, and attack it, without giving him time to change his pofition. This was the only probable means to bring their plan to bear. The method they took made it impracticable from the firft inftant they put the army in motion.

When the king quitted his camp with an air of precipitation, St. Germain fhould have followed him; and a ftrong detachment of cavalry have been fent on the road to Merfeburg, in order to reconnoitre his motions; and, if they found he was retiring, thefe two corps would have fufficed to beat his rear-guard; and, if it was found he only changed pofition, they would have kept him at bay, and give time to form the army, or retire into their old camp. Surely it was unpardonable to march with the whole army without any vanguard,

vanguard, which must never be done, particularly if near the enemy. When at length they were undeceived, and found that the enemy was forming on the heights of Reichertswerben, Why persist in advancing? They should instantly have formed their line as far backwards as possible, and by no means attempt it under the enemy's fire, and so near him; because such manœuvres can never succeed, if the enemy has either conduct or vigour.

THE king appears in a very different light: though he sees the enemy in motion all the morning, he is easy and quiet; no ways agitated, as too often is the case; waits 'till he perceives their intentions, and then instantly makes his dispositions. His marching behind the hill was attended with many great advantages: that appearance of a flight elated the spirits of the enemy so as to make them neglect the necessary precautions; they hastened so much that their army was thrown into some disorder while in march; and they were so perfectly deceived, that they found themselves, all at once, with the head of their columns, under the fire of the enemy's line; and so near, that they could not form their troops. The king saw this favourable moment, and ordered his cavalry to attack directly; and, though scarce any of the infantry was come up, he ordered those few battalions to advance before the enemy could make any disposition. One inch of ground, or one instant of time lost, would have given the enemy time and room to form their line; but the king's dispositions were so exact, and so well calculated, that neither happened; and he was most deservedly crowned with victory; which put an end to the campaign in Saxony.

WE have already said, that his majesty the king of Prussia, on leaving Lusatia, had left there the duke of Bevern,* with a
considerable

---

* Augustus William duke of Bevern was born in 1715: in 1733 he served against the French; in 1735 he entered the Prussian service, as lieutenant colonel; in 1739 he was made

considerable body of troops, to observe prince Charles; and, above all things, hinder him from making any solid enterprize against Silesia. Accordingly, the duke, having received a convoy from Bautzen, quitted Bernstadtel, and encamped on the mountain, called the Landscron, near Görlitz; and the better to secure the passes of the Neiss and Queiss, that he might enter Silesia, if necessary, he sent general Winterfield, with a strong corps, between those two rivers, at a place called Moys, near Görlitz.

Prince Charles advanced with the main army as far as Bernstadtel, and sent general Nadasti with a considerable corps to Seidenberg, also between the Neiss and Queiss, as well to observe Winterfield, as to secure a passage over the Neiss, and be ready to follow, or anticipate the duke of Bevern, whenever he went towards Silesia.

His royal highness was desirous to force the enemy to quit their present position, and carry the war into Silesia; because not only the army would be maintained at their expence, but, being much superior, could undertake something solid: whereas, if he continued there, the campaign would soon be at an end, and the fruits of their preceding good manœuvres lost. For these same reasons, it was incumbent on the duke of Bevern to keep things in the present

---

made a colonel, and wounded at the battle of Molwitz; in 1741 he had a regiment given him; in 1743 was made a major general; in 1747 governor of Stettin; in 1750 knight of the black eagle, and lieutenant general. He distinguished himself in the battles of Hohenfriedberg, Lowositz, Prague, Chotzemitz, and Breslaw: after which he was made a prisoner, while he went with a servant only to reconnoitre the enemy. He was in 1758 released, without any ransom, for his affinity to the empress. The king seeming offended at his conduct, he retired to his government of Stettin; where he remained 'till 1762; when he was called to the army in Silesia, and had a corps confided to him, while the king was besieging Schweidnitz. The Austrians, intending to relieve that place, attacked him with an army under the command of generals Lacy, Laudhon, and Odonell, whom he repulsed several times, though they were three times stronger than he was, and gave the king time to come to his aid. He may, no doubt, be numbered among the first generals of this age.

present situation, and draw on the war, without permitting the enemy to gain any considerable advantage. His position seemed to enable him to obtain this end. The Austrians could not, he thought, enter Silesia, and leave him behind, because he could return into Bohemia, and, by cutting off their subsistence, make it impossible for them to do any thing of consequence in Silesia; and, having a garrison in Bautzen, he was at hand likewise to favour, or be favoured, by the king's operations in Saxony; and, no doubt, could he have kept his position 'till the king had delivered that country from the combined army, the enemy must have been forced back into Bohemia, without even attempting any thing against Silesia.

Prince Charles, perfectly acquainted with all these reasons, resolved to force the enemy to quit their position, and march to Silesia; but, it having been judged too strong to be attacked, it was necessary to obtain by dint of proper manœuvres what could not be done by force. Wherefore, he sent a corps to drive the garrison out of Bautzen, and so cut off the enemy's communication with Saxony, and determined to attack general Winterfield, which would likewise cut them off from Silesia. These resolutions being taken, Nadasti's corps was considerably reinforced, and on the 7th of September the attack was made on that of Winterfield's. This general had posted, on a hill called Holtzberg, at a small distance from his camp, two battalions; against which the Austrians directed their attack, and came upon them before they could either be sustained or called back. They defended themselves with uncommon bravery; insomuch that Winterfield had time to come with some troops to their relief, and facilitate their retreat: upon which the combat became more violent than ever, in hopes of being able to keep their ground; but, having lost a great number of men, and their general mortally wounded, they were forced to quit their poft, and retire to their camp. The Auftrians took pofleffion of the Holtzberg; which, however, they abandoned the next morning; having loft, in this bloody action, killed and wounded, about 2000 men.

The duke of Bevern, having loft Bautzen, and with it his communication with the king in Saxony, and moreover fearing the Auftrians would now, after the defeat of Winterfield, pafs the Neifs with their main army, and fo hinder him from entering Silefia, refolved, while it was in his power, to march thither; and the more fo, as he could not poffibly fubfift in his prefent pofition, becaufe he could draw nothing from his magazines in Saxony, and what could be had from Silefia was fubject to be intercepted by the enemy's light troops, who were extremely numerous, and had a very favourable country, full of woods, ravins, hills, &c. to act in. Accordingly, not daring to pafs the Neifs at Görlitz, fo near the enemy, he fell down that river to Naumburg, and there paffed it; and from thence marched fucceffively, by Buntzlaw and Hainau, to Lignitz, where he arrived the 19th.

Prince Charles, having received information of the enemy's march, put his army inftantly in motion, and took his route by Lauban, Löwenberg, Goldberg, Hundorff, Jauer, Nicolftad, and Greibnig, where he arrived on the 25th. By taking this pofition he had cut off the enemy from Breflaw, Schweidnitz, and all Upper Silefia. On the following day, he ordered the village of Earfhdorff, where the enemy had pofted fome infantry, to be cannonaded; which, having put the houfes on fire, forced them to retire, and take a new pofition behind it, where they could be fuftained by the whole army. Prince Charles intended to attack them, but the duke of Bevern, propofing, if poffible, to regain his communication with Breflaw and Upper Silefia, quitted his

camp

camp in the night of the 27th, and directed his march towards Glogau, that he might pass the Oder in safety, if he was followed by the whole Austrian army; but, finding that only the vanguard pursued him, and that only on the right of the Katzbach, towards Parchwitz, he resolved to pass it near Lampersdorff; which was executed on the 29th; and, having marched up the right of the Oder, he repassed it at Breslaw, and on the 1st of October took his camp on the banks of the Lohe, with the city behind him. By this fine march he once more opened the communication with Upper Silesia, and covered the capital with his army, which was reciprocally covered by it.

PRINCE Charles found it would be useless to pursue the enemy on his quitting Lignitz, because he could only drive them under the cannon of Glogau, where they could remain in safety, and be provided with all the necessary stores and subsistence: whereas he, on the contrary, had no magazines in the country; nor could he form any, having the enemy in front, and their strong places behind him; so that he must necessarily fall back, and approach the frontiers of Bohemia; from whence only his numerous army could be nourished. For these reasons, instead of fatiguing his troops in a vain pursuit of the enemy, he directed his march towards Breslaw; hoping, no doubt, to take that place before the enemy could come near it, being in itself very weak, and moreover had then an inconsiderable garrison.

BEING arrived on the Schweidnitzwasser, a small river within three miles of Breslaw, he found the enemy had anticipated him, and was encamped, about two miles off, between him and that town. These circumstances made it necessary to concert new measures. His royal highness could not possibly continue long in that situation, as well for want of subsistence, as because the winter was growing sharp, and would soon make it impossible for him to

keep

keep the field; nor could he presume to separate his army in the middle of an enemy's country, where they had an army, and all the strong places, in their power. It seemed likewise rather dishonourable to retire into Bohemia without having attempted any thing, and so lose the fruits of their past labours; and the more so, as his army was much superior to that of the enemy already, and, besides, his royal highness expected a considerable body of Bavarians and Wurtemburgers, who were on their march, to join him. These motives made him determine to undertake the siege of some fortress, that he might have a place of arms in the enemy's country, and put part, at least, of his army in it, with safety, during the winter, and so be enabled to enter it the ensuing campaign without difficulty; and, having the necessary stores and provisions in this place, prosecute the war with more ease and safety than hitherto had been done.

This resolution being taken, the next object was, to fix upon the place that would best answer the end they had in view: Neifs, being near the frontiers of Moravia, could be attacked with more facility than any other; because they could be supplied with every thing necessary for such an undertaking from Olmutz, and the taking of it would secure a passage into Upper Silesia; and, besides, they would, the ensuing campaign, from thence attack the country of Glatz with more ease than from any other place whatever. To this it was objected, that Neifs was at such a distance, that the army could not arrive there 'till the season would be too far advanced to carry on the siege without infinite pains, and probably without success; and the more so, as the duke of Bevern could be there with his army long before them, and take such a position as would effectually cover the place; and lastly, that, though they should take it, the advantage that would accrue from it was trifling; because they would get scarce any part of the country with

it,

it; while the enemy had Kofel, Brieg, and Glatz, all about it; and that it only covered Moravia, leaving Bohemia quite open to the enemy.

IT was next propofed to attack the enemy before Breflaw: if they beat him, not only that fortrefs would fall, but they would be at liberty to attack any place in Upper Silefia; which, being left to their own weak garrifons, would foon be reduced: by this means the whole Auftrian army, covered by thefe places, could with fafety be feparated, and put into winter quarters. This propofition was very plaufible, but thought dangerous; becaufe, in cafe they did not fucceed in this attempt, it would be extreamly difficult to retire into Bohemia, from whence they were feparated by many high mountains, and had very bad roads to pafs through; and, moreover, the town of Schweidnitz, with a ftrong garrifon in it, behind them. Thefe reafons being well weighed, it was refolved to attack Schweidnitz, preferable to the two others abovementioned; becaufe they would be mafters of the principal defiles which lead to Bohemia on that fide, and of all the towns and villages behind Schweidnitz; which would enable them to keep the greateft part of the army in Silefia during the winter; and, moreover, if they took it without great lofs of time, they could then, with fafety, attack the duke of Bevern, having a place to retire to in cafe of misfortune, or undertake fome other enterprize.

ACCORDINGLY, general Nadafti, with a very confiderable corps, was fent to befiege Schweidnitz; where he was joined by the Bavarians and Wurtemburgers. This town lies in a fine plain, about three miles diftant from the mountains which feparate Silefia from Bohemia, is rich and populous: originally, when it firft came into the power of the Pruffians, during the preceding war, it was furrounded only by an old wall, with round towers, in the Gothic manner; but his majefty, confidering the advantageous fituation of

it,

it, as well to facilitate any projects he might hereafter form against Bohemia, as to cover Silesia, resolved to fortify it: accordingly, on the conclusion of that war, he ordered several redoubts, called star redoubts, because they resemble a star, to be built about it: these were joined by a curtain; and in the intervals, between the redoubts, were placed some small lunettes, or half moons: the whole covered by a ditch, with a covered way pallisaded.

Of all the species of works used in fortification, the starry redoubt is the worst; because, by the nature of its construction, it can have no flank; and the re-entering angles take up so much of the ground within, that they cannot contain the number of men and artillery sufficient to defend them; and are, moreover, exposed to be enfiladed from one end to the other; so that it is impossible they should make any considerable defence, when properly attacked.

General Nadasti ordered two true attacks, and one false one, to be made; and the trenches were opened in the night of the 27th of October; and, a breach having been made in three of these redoubts, the 11th at night, they were carried by assault; which forced the governor to capitulate the next morning. The garrison, consisting of 4 generals, and about 6000 men, were made prisoners of war: a vast quantity of provisions, artillery, and stores, were found in the place, and 300,000 florins.

During all this time, prince Charles, and the duke of Bevern, remained quiet in their camps by Breslaw; the first to cover the siege of Schweidnitz, and the other to fortify his camp; because he did not dare quit it, and march to relieve Schweidnitz, for fear of losing Breslaw, and be hemmed in between the prince's army, and that before Schweidnitz.

Prince Charles, having succeeded to his wish, in his undertaking against that place, was encouraged to attack the enemy, though now very strongly fortified; and, therefore, general Nadasti

was

was ordered to come and join the main army with that under his command. Accordingly, that general arrived on the 19th, and encamped on the right, as marked in the plan. The two following days were taken up in making the neceſſary preparations for the attack. Every thing being ready, on the 22d in the morning, the battle begun; of which we give here the different relations, as publiſhed by authority; which, with our reflections on the ground and the action, will be ſufficient to give a clear idea of it.

THAT publiſhed at Vienna is as follows:

" THE imperial and royal army was encamped, with the right
" at Strachwitz, and the left at Groſſmaſſelwitz, in two lines,
" and a reſerve. The grenadiers were poſted at Groſſmochber,
" to cover the right wing; and ſome regiments of infantry at
" Kleinmaſſelwitz, to cover the left. The army under general
" Nadaſti ſtood on our right, beyond Operau, on the left of the
" Lohe, with ſome light troops at Hartlieb, on the other ſide of
" it. The Pruſſian army was likewiſe poſted in two lines; the
" infantry in the firſt, and the cavalry in the ſecond; both ex-
" tending from Coſel to Kleinmochber, and from thence, in a
" ſtrait line, towards Breſlaw; ſo that it formed a half ſquare,
" with the angle at Kleinmochber: but, when they perceived our
" diſpoſitions, they changed their poſition, and that part of the
" army which extended from Kleinmochber towards Breſlaw, was
" ordered to advance towards the Lohe, and occupy ſome hills,
" as well as the villages of Kleinburg and Kreitern, in order to
" make a front againſt general Nadaſti. They were covered by
" the Lohe, which is not broad, but the banks of it are very
" marſhy; and had thrown up a great many redoubts and re-
" trenchments. Their right wing was covered by an abatis, or
" parapet of trees cut down; behind which they had poſted their

" h nters

" hunters or markfmen, and fix battalions of grenadiers, to cover
" their right flank. The village of Pilfnitz, through which the
" Lohe paffes, was well fortified with redoubts, before and behind
" it, which prefented continually fome new defence. The fame
" was done at the villages of Schmiedfeld, Hoflichen, Klein-
" mochber, and Grabifchen, with breaftworks, ditches, and three
" rows of wolf-holes;* fo that it was almoft impoffible to pafs
" them. Befides thefe works, there were likewife, between and
" behind the villages, other redoubts and batteries, with parapets,
" as far as the fuburbs of the town. On the other fide the Oder
" they had put fome infantry in the villages of Protfch, Weida,
" Hunnern, Simfdorff, and Rofenthal; and fome cavalry between
" the villages. Upon the left wing they had moreover two re-
" giments of Huffars.

" Such was the fituation of both armies: the Auftrian amounted
" to 60,000 men, and the Pruffian to about 40,000.

" In confequence of the meafures concerted between his royal
" highnefs and his excellency marfhal Daun, batteries were raifed
" the 21ft at night, the pontoons brought near the places where
" the bridges were to be laid, and all the other neceffary prepa-
" rations for paffing the river and attacking the enemy's works
" being compleated, the army marched the 22d, before day, and
" was formed, in two lines, on the banks of the Lohe; the firft
" was compofed of infantry, and the other of cavalry. The bag-
" gage was fent back behind the Schweidnitz, and the furgeons
" ordered to follow the army, and to ftay at certain places, where
" the wounded were to be brought.

" The 22d, the day appointed for the attack, there was a great
" fog, which prevented us from feeing the enemy's difpofitions.
" At

---

* Round holes, generally about two feet in diameter at the top, one at the bottom, and near two deep.

"At nine in the morning we raised four batteries, in which 40 pieces of cannon were placed, which played on the villages of Pilsnitz, Schmiedfeld, Hoflichen, Kleinmochber and Grabischen, and the redoubts, 'till 12 o'clock. In the mean while, the fog began to dissipate; upon which we advanced to lay the bridges over the river; and, in less than three quarters of an hour, seven were made in the enemy's presence, and under their fire.

"His royal highness and M. Daun were at Grossinochber, and the signal agreed upon being given by their orders, general Sprecher, who had under his orders major general Richlin, advanced with 35 companies of grenadiers, sustained by 12 companies of horse grenadiers, commanded by prince Lowenstein, and passed the bridge by Grossmochber. These troops were supported by the right wing of the first line of infantry, under the command of lieutenant general Andlau, and major generals duke of Ursel, and baron Unrhue; and, moreover, by the corps de reserve, commanded by lieutenant generals count Wied, and Nicholas Esterhasi, and major generals Blonquet, Wolf, and Otterwolf; and, lastly, by the right wing of the second line, commanded by lieutenant generals Minulph, count Stahremberg, and major generals Wulfen, and Buttler.

"At the same time and place, count Luchesi, general of horse, and lieutenant generals Spada, and Wolwart, and major generals Deville, Kolbel, and Aspremont, with the right wing of the first line of horse, likewise passed. All these troops formed, in two lines, on the other side the Lohe, under the fire of the enemy's artillery, and attacked their cavalry and infantry that were advancing. At 1 o'clock the fire of the small arms began, and lasted very hot, and in good order, about half an hour, without being able to force either side to cede an inch.

"At laſt, the enemy's horſe and foot were obliged to give way; upon which our infantry took the village of Grabiſchen, and the great battery behind it. Our troops advanced ſtill forwards to the retrenchment by Kleinmochber; and, though the enemy had ſent there both infantry and artillery, they were, however, drove further back.

"The next attack was commanded by lieutenant general count Arberg, and under him major general Lacy, and was ſuſtained by the infantry, commanded by lieutenant general Macquire, and by the left wing of the ſecond line of horſe, commanded by count Stambach, general of horſe. This column was to attack the villages of Schmiedfeld and Hoflichen; and, at 3 o'clock paſſed the Lohe. Counts Arberg and Macquire attacked the redoubts by Schmiedfeld, and, after a moſt bloody combat, drove the enemy out of them. At the ſame time, count Wied, who commanded the reſerve, advanced againſt Hoflichen; and, notwithſtanding it was covered by breaſtworks, ditches, and wolfholes, he took it; as well as the redoubt that was near it.

"The third attack againſt Pilſnitz was more violent, and laſted longer than any of the others. This village is cut in two by the Lohe, whoſe banks are very high here, and the ground all about is very cloſe and difficult to be paſſed; and, beſides, the entry and the iſſue out of it were covered by redoubts. General Keuhl, with the left wing of infantry, ſuſtained by the left wing of the ſecond line of horſe, commanded by count Serbelloni, was ordered to attack this village, and the neighbouring works; but, by the difficulty of the ground, the ſtrength of the works, and the bravery of the enemy, he was repulſed, with great loſs, three ſeveral times. At laſt, however, though it was now near ſix o'clock, and quite dark, he renewed the attack with ſo much courage and bravery, that the

"enemy

"enemy was forced to give way, and abandon fucceffively the
" village and the redoubts.

" WE thought that, with the day, the battle was likewife at
" an end. The enemy, however, appeared again, and a column
" advanced againft Kleinmochber, endeavouring to come on the
" flank of the archduke Jofeph's and Leopold's regiments of horfe..
" Thefe being fuftained by fix companies of grenadiers, poſted in
" the redoubts, commanded by general Sprecher, made fuch good
" manœuvres, as kept the enemy at a diftance, till prince Charles's
" regiment of foot, and Luchefi's regiment of horfe, had time to
" come up, which obliged them to retire for good and all.

" NOT far from Pilfnitz, on the right of the Lohe, the enemy,
" had a great abatis, which reached quite to the Oder. Colonel
" Brentano, with his Croats, fuftained by 1000 men of regular
" infantry, was ordered to attack it. He had the good fortune
" to fucceed, and pafs it; but, as we had not then got poſſeſſion
" of Pilfnitz, he was forced to retire with fome lofs. Soon after,
" however, he renewed the attack; and, as our left wing was
" then advanced to Pilfnitz, he paffed the abatis, and threw the
" enemy into no fmall confufion.

" MAJOR general Beck, with a confiderable corps, was fent
" over the Oder; and, having drove the enemy out of feveral vil-
" lages they occupied, he cannonaded the enemy's right wing,
" over the Oder, at Cofel, in flank and rear.

" WHAT we have hitherto related was performed by the army,
" which had always remained in this neighbourhood during the
" fiege of Schweidnitz. Befides thefe feveral attacks, general Na-
" dafti, with the army he had commanded at the above fiege,
" (excepting a few battalions) and reinforced by four regiments
" of horfe, was ordered to divide his troops in three columns,
" at the head of which were the grenadiers, fuftained by battalions

" and.

"and brigades, and having paſſed the Lohe, to attack the ene-
"my's left wing, that was poſted againſt him. Accordingly, he
"occupied the village of Hartlieb the 21ſt, which the enemy
"held with infantry and cavalry; and, on the 22d, at break of
"day, he paſſed the Lohe, and formed his army with the right
"at Oltaſchin, and the left towards Kreitern, where the artillery
"of reſerve was likewiſe poſted. The enemy, whoſe cavalry ex-
"tended on the plains of Durjahn, endeavoured to take our corps
"in the flank, which the good diſpoſitions of general Nadaſti
"prevented.

"In the mean time, general Wolferſdorff, with 16 companies
"of grenadiers, attacked the village of Kleinburg, drove the ene-
"my out of it, took one cannon, and advanced to Woiſchwitz.
"The Saxon light horſe, who were on the right, were preparing
"to advance; but, the evening coming on, and the enemy's horſe
"being advantageouſly poſted on a hill, behind ſome redoubts,
"general Nadaſti thought it would be needleſs to attempt any
"thing farther.

"During this time, the enemy attacked Kleinburg with ſeven
"battalions, and ſome cavalry; and, having put it on fire, retired
"on the hills behind the redoubts; where they continued 'till
"they found that the reſt of their army was retiring; then they
"followed them, and paſſed the Oder, through Breſlaw. We
"have taken 36 pieces of cannon, and about 600 men priſoners,
"with above 3000 deſerters."

The Pruſſians account of this battle is very little exact; particularly where it ſays, that the Auſtrian's right wing had not only
been repulſed, but that it quitted the field, and retired to Neumark, many miles off; which is both falſe and ridiculous. It is
as follows:

"When

" WHEN the Auftrians had taken Schweidnitz, and the corps
" employed in that fiege had joined the main army at Liffa, they
" refolved to attack the prince of Bevern's corps before the king
" could come to fuccour him. They knew that, in fpite of
" Marfhall's and Haddick's corps, he had already paffed through
" Lufatia. Accordingly, on the 22d of November, the attack
" was made, at nine in the morning. The enemy's army was, at
" leaft, three times ftronger than ours, as appears by the gazettes
" they have often publifhed : and general Nadafti had a particu-
" lar corps oppofite the flank of our left wing. The attack fuc-
" ceeded fo ill to the Auftrians, that their right wing was totally
" defeated, and forced to retire towards Neumark. Lieutenant
" general Ziethen, who commanded our left wing, likewife en-
" tirely defeated Nadafti's corps, and the enemy thought the bat-
" tle loft; having been forced, in moft places, to fly ; but, as on
" our right fome of our regiments had fomewhat fuffered, the
" prince of Bevern thought it beft to quit the field of battle,
" which we had kept till 5 o'clock, and retire into our camp,
" and the following night to pafs the Oder, over the bridge that
" is in the town of Breflaw. The Auftrians, finding that every
" thing was abandoned as far as Breflaw, returned, and occupied
" the field of battle; which, to their great aftonifhment, we had
" quitted. Our lofs is midling : that of the Auftrians, according
" to accounts worthy of credit, amounts to above 20,000 men.
" The 23d we remained behind Breflaw. The 24th, the duke
" of Bevern rode out at 4 o'clock in the morning, with one fer-
" vant only, in order to reconnoitre the enemy, and fell in with
" fome of their advanced pofts, who made him prifoner. The
" fame day, having waited in vain the duke's return, lieutenant
" general Kyow took upon him the command of the army. Ge-
" neral Leftewitz, who, by the king's orders, was left commander

" of

"of Breslaw, could not possibly defend long so extensive a place, and so ill fortified, against such a considerable army as that of the enemy; and so he must be content to have leave to retire, with his garrison, and the sick we had left in Breslaw, to Glogau."

The Austrians lost in this action 666, among which one general, killed: 4620, of which five generals, wounded: 437 missing: and about 400 horses killed, wounded, and lost.

No account appeared of the loss of the Prussians.

REFLECTIONS on the battle of Breslaw, and the preceding operations.

It has been already observed, that there is, in every camp, some one essential point, or hinge, which may be called the key of it, and on which the strength of it most immediately depends: the same holds good as to positions. In a whole country there may not, perhaps, be one found which will enable a general to obtain his ends. The choice of this point, with regard to positions, depends entirely on, and must be regulated by, the object he has in view; by the situation of his magazines; and by the number and species of his troops; that he may not only have a good position, but likewise a good field of battle, in case he is attacked.

The duke of Bevern had two objects in view: the first and principal one was to cover Silesia; and particularly Breslaw, Schweidnitz, and Neiss; against which alone the enemy could direct their operations: the other object was only secondary, and of much less consequence; and was to keep open a communication with the Elbe, as well to act in concert with the king in Saxony, as because he drew his subsistence chiefly from Dresden. The camp he had taken at Bernstadtel, though a little too far back, answered, in some measure, these ends: he could be on the Elbe,

or

or in Silefia, fooner than the enemy, by marching on his right, by Lôbau and Bautzen; or on his left, by Lauban and Löwenberg, and fo on to Schweidnitz or Breflaw. The only inconveniency of this pofition, was, that the enemy, being much fuperior, could fend ftrong corps towards Bautzen, and thereby render his convoys, coming from the Elbe, precarious. This, however, might have been remedied by occupying Bautzen with a confiderable detachment of cavalry, and fome light infantry, and pofting another of the fame fpecies about Lôbau; which would have formed a chain from his right quite to the Elbe; fo that he might, and, as we think, ought to have kept this pofition as long as poffible; which would have ftopped the progrefs of the enemy.

INSTEAD of which, he abandoned it, and took another, ftill farther back, on the Landfcron, near Görlitz: the confequence of which was, that he inftantly loft his communication with the Elbe, and rendered that with Silefia very difficult; nor could he remain in his prefent fituation for want of fubfiftence: he might, however, ftill have anticipated the enemy's march into Silefia, and towards Breflaw and Schweidnitz, if, inftead of marching by Langenau, Naumburg, Buntzlaw, Hainau, and Lignitz, he had marched by Lauban, Löwenberg, Goldberg, and Jauer; which the king did, the year following, after the battle of Hochkirchen, in much more difficult circumftances: for the whole Auftrian army was encamped on the Landfcron, within fight; yet he paffed the Neifs and Queifs, and, in fpite of the enemy, went into Upper Silefia, and raifed the fiege of Neifs. If, therefore, the prince of Bevern had taken this route, and even gone to Liebenthal, between Greiffenberg and Löwenberg, with a ftrong corps on the right of the Queifs, between Markliffa and Grieffenberg, it would have been impoffible for the enemy to advance one ftep farther: they could not pafs between his left and thofe immenfe mountains,

R called

called the Riefengeburg, having no road; much lefs could they march on his right, towards Löwenberg and Lignitz, leaving him mafter of thofe immenfe defiles and mountains which feparated them from Bohemia, from whence only they could draw their fubfiftence, without expofing their army to certain deftruction. They muft, therefore, either ftop fhort, or come to an action; which he could accept, much to his advantage, in that ftrong camp of Liebenthal, or decline it, and retire fucceffively to Lahn and Jauer, and laftly to Striegau and Schweidnitz. In all which places there are fuch camps to be taken, as cannot eafily be forced. The country is extremely clofe, and therefore numbers are of little ufe, becaufe they cannot be all brought to action: whereas, by taking the march he did, he left that very road open which he ought to have taken, and by that means gave the enemy an opportunity to anticipate him; fo that, on his arrival at Lignitz, he found they had taken a pofition between that town and Jauer, and by that means cut him off from Schweidnitz, Neifs, Breflaw, and all Upper Silefia. Indeed he got afterwards to Breflaw, but this ought to be attributed to his extraordinary good fortune, that the enemy committed a greater fault than he had done. Being arrived at Breflaw, we think he ought to have drawn the principal effects and ftores out of it, and fent them to Glogau, and have gone with his army to Schweidnitz, where the enemy muft have followed him; becaufe they could not keep Breflaw, even if they had taken it while he was mafter of Schweidnitz, and of the defiles which lead into Bohemia; nor could they force him, by any manœuvre, to abandon that town, and the neighbourhood; nor, fuppofing they were mafters of Breflaw, could they put their army into winter quarters, while he was in poffeffion of a chain of fortreffes behind them, and had an army between them and their own country, with which they could not have the leaft communication, not even with

the

the capital; fo that they muft neceffarily be forced to quit Silefia, and endeavour to gain Bohemia; which was by no means an eafy undertaking; becaufe, as we have faid, they were feparated from that country by an enemy's army, and three ftrong fortreffes, as Schweidnitz, Glatz, and Neifs, on the very defiles where they muft pafs; and, in which, in all human probability, their army, in that advanced feafon, and harraffed by the enemy, would have perifhed. By ftaying at Breflaw, and fuffering Schweidnitz to be taken, he gave prince Charles an opportunity to take firft a poft in the country, and by that means enabled him to profecute his advantages with fecurity; which brought on the lofs of the battle of Breflaw, and with it Breflaw itfelf; and might, if thefe advantages had been properly improved, occafioned that of all Silefia.

WHENEVER the Auftrians attempt any thing againft that country, by the way of Lufatia, the Pruffians may, we think, by taking the above pofitions, even with an inconfiderable army, effectually ftop their progrefs.

As to the conduct of the action of Breflaw, we think that the Pruffians, to the many works, which, during feven weeks, they had raifed, fhould have added an inundation, if poffible, by means of the Lohe. This would have effectually covered them. The choice of the camp does not appear to have been well made; becaufe the left wing and its flank were not fo ftrong as the front; fo that, if the enemy had made the principal attack where Nadafti was, the Pruffians muft have abandoned their ftrong camp, and lofe the fruits of their long labours, in order to make a front where Ziethen ftood; and, moreover, if the enemy ever got poffeffion of the hills behind Kleinburg and Grabifchen, the whole Pruffian army would have been hemmed in between the Lohe and the Oder, with general Beck in their rear on the other fide, and the enemy in front, without fufficient ground to manœuvre upon;

and, in such circumstances, it would have been difficult even to get into Breslaw. It would, I think, have been better to place the right on the town of Breslaw, and occupy the villages that were near and under the protection of it. The left should have been extended to the hills by Kleinburg and Grabischen, which ought to have been fortified with care, and redoubts raised all along the front, from right to left. The army, so posted, could not, we think, have been forced at all; nor could the town be attacked while it was there. When the enemy passed the Lohe at Großmochber, we think that general Ziethen, instead of extending his left, should, on the contrary, have lengthened his right as far as Grabischen, with his infantry and all the heavy artillery on the hill it, and his cavalry at the bottom of it; and the prince of Bevern's division should have closed its left with the right of this. By which means, the enemy, who had passed the Lohe there, would have been taken in flank, whether they attacked Grabischen or Kleinmochber: whereas, by the dispositions made, there was an interval between Ziethen's right, and the prince of Bevern's left, where the enemy entered, and met with no other difficulty than that at Kleinmochber. This interval was the key of the camp; and, the instant the enemy got possession of it, the prince of Bevern could not continue where he was, though he had been victorious on his right and center; because, being masters of this interval, if they reinforced that attack, which they might have done, they were on his flank, and would successively have pushed him into the Oder: whereas, if he repulsed the enemy here, the battle was won; because, though they succeeded in their attacks at Pilsnitz and Schmiedfeld, they could not continue in that ground between the Lohe, the Oder, and his army, with Breslaw just before them; and must, therefore, have abandoned those villages, and repass the Lohe.

THE

THE event confirms my opinion: for the enemy had got no very great advantage on the right and center; yet it was neceſſary to retire, becauſe they had taken Grabifchen and Kleinmochber, and were, confequently, on prince Bevern's flank; and might, if he continued in the fame poſition, cut him off from Breſlaw, and throw him into the Oder.

As to the conduct of prince Charles, it ſeems to have been no leſs prudent than vigorous. By ſending two corps on the enemy's flank, he forced them to quit their ſtrong camp on the Landſcron, and go farther down, in order to paſs the Neifs and Queifs; which was an eſſential advantage to him, becauſe he had, by that means, a nearer road than they to Breſlaw and Schweidnitz. When his royal highneſs came to Lignitz, we think he ſhould have attacked the enemy; and, if that was thought dangerous, he ſhould have ſent 20,000 men to beſiege Breſlaw, then defended by a very weak garriſon; and, with the remainder of the army, have covered the ſiege; which he could eaſily have done, being ſtill very much ſuperior to the enemy, who could not poſſibly approach Breſlaw, without previouſly coming to an action.

WHEN the prince of Bevern quitted Lignitz, and marched towards Steinau, on the Oder, prince Charles ſhould have ſent a ſtrong corps after him, and with the army have gone to Dyherrenfurth; and there throw as many bridges as poſſible over the Oder, in order to be on either ſide, as circumſtances might require. By this means he could cover the ſiege of Breſlaw, and effectually hinder the enemy from diſturbing it. Why he permitted the prince of Bevern to march near twenty leagues, and paſs the Oder twice, and come to Breflaw before him, while he had only ten leagues to march, and no river to paſs, is what cannot eaſily be conceived. As to the conduct of the action itſelf, it does not ſeem to have been intirely prudent and blameleſs. The three attacks were made preciſely againſt the ſtrongeſt part of the enemy's camp,

and

and were, moreover, expofed to great difficulties in paffing the Lohe under the fire of their works: whereas, if his royal highnefs had only made a falfe attack on the enemy's center and right, and have pofted his left by Neukirchen, with fome heavy artillery and haubitz near it, and have paffed his line by Groffmochber, between Operau and the Lohe, where the bridges muft have been laid, and Nadafti's left quite clofe to the prince's right, fo as to form a kind of curve about the enemy, as marked in the plan, he would have avoided the villages and works, in which the enemy placed the greateft hopes, and the difficulties that muft occur in paffing a river fo near them; and, moreover, would have forced them to abandon thefe very works, in order to take a new pofition, with their right on the Lohe, and their left towards the hills behind Kleinburg, which would have expofed it to be enfiladed from one end to the other, by the artillery placed at Neukirchen and Groffmochber. When the enemy's right and center quitted their ground, as they muft have done, nothing could hinder the light troops from occupying it, and taking them in the rear. For all which reafons, I think, the Auftrians fhould have made their attack where Nadafti was, by which they would have avoided all thofe great difficulties they met with. Even, if this general, inftead of extending his right, had ftretched his left fo as to clofe with the right of the army which paffed at Groffmochber, and have acted with his ufual vigour, it is probable the Pruffian army was loft, and thrown into the Oder.

The immediate confequence of this battle was the taking of Breflaw, with about 300,000 florins, and a prodigious quantity of ftores in it.

The Auftrians, thinking the campaign finifhed, were preparing to enter into winter quarters; when news came, that the king, at the head of a confiderable body of troops, was advancing towards Silefia.

in GERMANY, 1757. 127

Silefia. Upon which all thoughts of feparating the army were laid afide, and proper meafures taken to go and oppofe the enemy. With this view, colonel Bulow, with about 3000 men, was fent to occupy Lignitz, in hopes, by that means, to ftop the king for fome time; as it was thought he would pafs near that place. Prince Charles, having refolved to go and meet the enemy, paffed the Schweidnitz on the 4th of December, intending to advance further on towards Glogau; but the arrival of the enemy, the day following, prevented it, and occafioned a general action, near Liffa: of which we fhall, as ufual, give the different accounts, as publifhed by authority.

THAT of the Auftrians is as follows:

" THE king of Pruffia, having quitted Saxony, and paffed
" through Lufca, he arrived, with a confiderable corps, at
" Parchwitz, on the Oder, where he was joined by the army
" which had been under the command of the prince of Bevern;
" which, with what he had conducted, amounted to 40,000 men,
" provided with a fine train of artillery, fafcines, gabions, &c.
" and, having paffed the Katzbach, it was eafy to forefee that his
" intentions were to take Neumark and Lignitz; and then, either
" attack the imperial army before Breflaw, or march to Striegau
" and the frontiers of Bohemia, in order to cut off our communi-
" cation with that country.

" FOR which reafons, it was refolved by his royal highnefs
" prince Charles, and his excellency M. Daun, with the unanimous
" confent of all the generals, to advance, and pafs the Schweidnitz
" without delay, and fo fecure Lignitz; and, above all things,
" endeavour to fruftrate the defigns of the enemy. Accordingly,
" the garrifon of Lignitz was reinforced, and a large corps of
" Bannalifts, huffars and picquets of horfe, fuftained by the Saxon
" light horfe, were fent to Neumark.

" THE

"The army, having been provided on the 3d of December,
"for four days, with every thing necessary, and prepared for all
"events, broke up the 4th in the morning, and passed the Lohe
"and the Schweidnitz, in order to encamp there. While it was
"filing over the bridges, advice was brought, that the king of
"Prussia had quitted Parchwitz the 4th in the morning, and was
"advanced to Neumark, from whence he had forced our troops
"to retire. Upon which the baggage was sent back behind the
"Schweidnitz, and the columns ordered to hasten their march,
"that the army might be formed; which was accordingly done,
"in two lines. General Nadasti, with the corps under his com-
"mand, made a third, which was designed to cover the flank of
"the left wing; and the corps de reserve that of the right. The
"army was posted with the right at Nypern, the left at Leuthen,
"and the center at Frobelwitz: all these villages were occupied
"with infantry, and provided with artillery. In Frobelwitz were
"eight companies of granadiers, with many picquets: in Leuthen
"seven companies of granadiers, with several picquets: and seve-
"ral picquets also in Nypern. All the companies of granadiers,
"and the picquets of the reserve, were posted on the right of the
"cavalry, at the point of a wood that joined it.

"General Lusinski, with two regiments of hussars, and some
"granitzers, sustained by the Saxon light horse, commanded by
"count Nostitz, was posted so as to cover the left wing; and
"general Morocz, with two regiments of hussars, and some gra-
"nitzers, on the right, for the same purpose. Whilst we were
"making these dispositions, the enemy advanced on this side Neu-
"mark, with his right at Krintfch, and the left at Bifchdorff,
"with his foreposts at Borna. In this situation both armies con-
"tinued under arms the whole night. The 5th in the morning,
"before day, general Nadasti, whose corps had made a third line,

"went,

" went, as had been concerted, and pofted himfelf near the ca-
" valry of the left wing, and extended his troops to a hill, that
" was on the fide, upon which fome artillery was placed, and an
" abatis made before it. The Auftrians under his command
" were next the left of the army, and the Wurtemburgers and
" Bavarians came to be on the flank, and behind the abatis.

" At break of day, the enemy made feveral motions, fometimes
" to the right, and fometimes to the left, which lafted 'till 12
" o'clock; and it appeared he intended to attack the right wing
" of the imperial army; infomuch that general Luchefi, who
" commanded there, fent feveral times to demand fuccours. The
" referve was deftined for that purpofe; yet the fending of it
" was poftponed 'till the enemy's intentions were fully known:
" but, as the count repeated his inftances, and the enemy's mo-
" tions behind the hills not being difcovered, the referve was fent
" him, and M. Daun went there himfelf, in order to be at hand
" in cafe of need. Scarce had the referve marched, when the
" enemy's cavalry appeared on our left; which fhewed they pro-
" pofed attacking that wing, and the flank adjoining: upon which
" his royal highnefs and his excellency M. Daun ordered prince
" Efterhafi, general of horfe, and generals Macquire and Angern,
" with the cavalry and infantry under their command, and all the
" fecond line, to march and fuftain that flank. About 1 o'clock
" the enemy approached it, and the fire of the fmall arms began
" againft the Wurtembergers; which being very hot, forced them
" back in confufion, leaving their artillery behind them; which
" brought the Bavarians, who formed the flank, likewife into
" confufion. Thefe auxiliary troops immediately threw the other
" regiments of the Imperials in diforder, and hindered thofe that
" were coming to fuftain them from doing any thing to the purpofe.
" Every poffible means was ufed to bring the troops into order,

" but

"but in vain. During this time, the enemy attacked the village
"of Leuthen, and the left wing of the army, and had brought
"there the greatest part of his forces; but he was repulsed three
"several times with great loss; so that the victory was dubious
"for a long while. At length, however, the Prussians penetrated
"in the opening between the left wing and the flank, and so
"were in the rear of our army. We were forced to abandon
"Leuthen, and retire towards the Schweidnitz and the Lohe.
"This was executed in good order, and under a continual fire.
"In this manner the battle, which lasted from 1 o'clock 'till
"five, finished."

The Prussian's account is as follows:

"After the battle of Rosbach, his majesty turned his thoughts
"towards Silesia, in order to oppose vigorously the progress of
"the Austrians. Accordingly, his majesty, at the head of 33
"squadrons, and 19 battalions, quitted Leipsig the 12th of No-
"vember, and arrived the 13th at Eulenberg, the 14th at Tor-
"gau, the 16th at Muhlberg, the 17th passed the Roder at
"Grossenhayn, where general Haddick had been with 2000 men,
"but was retired to Konigsbruck. He had left some hussars be-
"hind the Roder to observe us; but they were drove back by
"ours, who took about 40 prisoners.

"The 18th his majesty marched by Polsnitz to Konigsbruck,
"where the pandours under general Haddick stopped once more;
"whom he forced to retire towards the corps under general Mar-
"shal, in Lusatia, who likewise retired towards Lôbau, and ne-
"ver appeared again during our whole march. The 20th his
"majesty passed over the Black Elster to Camenz; and the 21st
"over the Spree to Bautzen; from whence Marshal's corps had
"retired towards Bohemia: the 22d his majesty passed the Old
"Spree, and went to Maltitz; the 23d to Gorlitz; from whence
" Haddick's

" Haddick's corps likewife retired towards Bohemia: the 24th
" he paffed the Queifs, and went to Naumburg in Silefia; the
" 26th to Deutmanfdorff; the 27th to Lobethau; and the 28th
" to Parchwitz; where we arrived at 6 o'clock in the evening,
" and there found the Auftrian colonel Gerfdorff, who was juft
" come with about 1100 horfe and foot. His majefty ordered
" him to be immediately attacked, and killed about 80 men, took
" 150 prifoners, and difperfed the reft. The army paffed the
" Katzbach, and remained fome days at Parchwitz, to reft after
" fuch a ftrong march. The 1ft of December, the huffars, be-
" longing to the army of prince Bevern, came to us; and the 2d
" that whole army joined ours. On the 4th we marched to Neu-
" mark, where we found fome thoufand Croats and huffars, who
" kept the gate oppofite to us fhut, and endeavoured to get out
" on the fide of Breflaw. In the mean while, fome of our dra-
" goons and huffars went about the town, and others opened the
" gate by force; fo that, having drove the enemy out, they fell
" into the hands of thofe who had gone on the other fide. We
" killed about 300, and took 600 prifoners, with the bakery of
" the whole army, a fmall magazine, and two cannon. Here ad-
" vice was brought, that prince Charles had quitted Breflaw, and
" was advanced to Liffa, with his right at Nypern, and his left at
" Golau, with the Schweidnitz behind him. His majefty thought
" proper to go and meet him; and therefore ordered the army to
" break up on the 5th, at 5 o'clock in the morning. At break of
" day we difcovered, on a hill behind the village of Borna, about
" half a mile from Neumark, a ftrong corps of cavalry, which, in
" the twilight, was thought to be the enemy's whole army. Upon
" our approaching them, we found it was only two regiments of
" huffars, and the Saxon light horfe, commanded by general
" Noftitz. Our vanguard attacked them immediately; drove
" them

" them back into their camp; and took 500 prisoners. We
" continued our march, in wet and thick weather, about four
" miles; and, near 12 o'clock, we discovered the enemy's whole
" army, in order of battle, behind the village of Leuthen. All
" the hills before their front were covered with artillery; and
" the left wing had, besides a great hill with artillery upon it,
" an abatis likewise. The right had also a great many batteries
" before it. The king resolved to attack the enemy's left, as
" soon as our army reached the heights before it. We marched on
" the right; so that our right wing came up to the Schweidnitz
" river. We first attacked the wood; and very soon drove the
" enemy's infantry out of it. When they perceived that we out-
" winged them, and took them in flank, they were forced to
" change their position; and, as we were on their flank, they had
" nothing more to do, than to take the first new position they
" could find, to hinder us from enfilading their army from one
" wing to the other. They therefore sent some brigades of in-
" fantry on the heights abovementioned, behind the wood: our
" right wing attacked it; and, after an obstinate combat, took
" it. The enemy formed a new line by Leuthen, and defended
" themselves with much bravery; but, at last, were forced to
" give way. Here our cavalry of the right wing attacked that
" of the enemy, and defeated it. They were, however, afterwards
" drove back by the enemy's artillery charged with cartridges:
" but, being again re-established, they attacked their infantry,
" and took many prisoners. During these several attacks, the
" enemy's right advanced. The cavalry of our left attacked that
" of the enemy, and entirely defeated it: then our regiment of
" dragoons Bareuth attacked a body of infantry, that was on a
" hill, behind, while our infantry did the same in front; which
" soon forced them to fly. His majesty pursued the enemy to
                                                " Lissa.

" Liſſa. The battle began at 1 o'clock, and finiſhed at four.
" If we had had a few hours more day light, the enemy's loſs
" would have been ſtill much greater. Prince Maurice com-
" manded the right wing under the king, and major general Ret-
" zow the left. Our loſs confiſts in 500 men killed, and 2300
" wounded: among theſe is general Rochow, who was alſo taken
" priſoner. The enemy's army, which amounted to 80,000 men,
" never fought with more bravery than this time. Ours amounted
" to 36,000 men only. The enemy ſtood in a plain, with ſome
" ſmall hills on it, which they covered with artillery. There
" were likewiſe many buſhes on the plain, of which they took
" advantage. On their left wing was a confiderable wood, where
" they made an abatis, and took all the meaſures poſſible to hin-
" der us from coming on their flank. General Nadaſti, with his
" corps, was likewiſe poſted there, with intention to come on
" our flank. For which reaſon, his majeſty placed four battalions
" behind the cavalry of our right; which wiſe difpofition was
" afterwards of great ſervice to us: for, when Nadaſti attacked our
" right wing of horſe, and had thrown ſome regiments in con-
" fuſion, the fire of theſe battalions threw the enemy back in
" great diſorder, and by that means cleared our flank, and ena-
" bled our right to act with vigour againſt the enemy's left, which
" in a ſhort time was forced to retire. The right wing of our
" infantry continued to advance in the fineſt order, though it was
" expoſed to a prodigious cannonading, and the fire of ſmall arms.
" Our artillery, of which we had no ſmall quantity, did great
" ſervice, and ſuſtained our advancing infantry; and by degrees
" ſilenced that of the enemy, which was at laſt abandoned.
" Though the enemy had fought with great bravery during the
" whole action, yet they ſeemed to redouble their forces and
" courage at Leuthen, which was fortified with redoubts and
                                            " retrenchments,

" retrenchments. The combat lasted here above an hour; and
" our brave battalions made several attacks, one after another,
" before they got masters of the village. This decided the battle;
" for the enemy, on losing this village, retired with great pre-
" cipitation, and never attempted again to make any considerable
" stand. Our cavalry, and particularly the hussars, pursued the
" flying enemy; killed many; and took some thousands prisoners.
" His majesty pursued the enemy to Lissa, where he ordered the
" army to remain that night under arms. Our infantry did won-
" ders. We thought, in the beginning, that our left would have
" no opportunity to come to action, as our right advanced so
" much before it; however, at 4 o'clock, the battle was gene-
" ral: even our small reserve was ordered to advance into the
" line. Our cavalry had many difficulties, in the beginning, to
" encounter, from the ditches and enclosures: at last, how-
" ever, by the activity of our brave general Ziethen, it had also
" an opportunity of acting. The 6th we followed the enemy,
" and the 7th invested Breslaw. General Ziethen, with a great
" corps of infantry and cavalry, was sent after them. He has
" taken several cannons, and above 3000 waggons. We have
" taken, in and since the battle, to the 12th of December, 291
" officers, and 21,500 men, prisoners, among whom are generals
" Nostitz, and Odonell, 116 cannon, 51 pair of colours, and 4000
" waggons."

The loss of the Austrians, not including the Wurtembergers and Bavarians, amounted to 6574, killed and wounded. Among the first were generals Luchesi, Otterwolf, and prince Stolberg: and among the wounded were generals Haller, Macquire, Lacy, Lobkowitz, and Preysac. That of the Prussians consisted of about 5000 men, not including the cavalry.

Prince

PRINCE Charles left a very confiderable garrifon in Breflaw, under the command of general Sprecher, and retired to Schweidnitz; and, having provided for the defence of that place, he made his difpofitions to retire into Bohemia; which was accordingly executed: and, before the end of the month, the Auftrians entirely evacuated Silefia, excepting only the town of Schweidnitz.

IN the mean time, the king opened the trenches before Breflaw; and, a bomb having fallen into a powder magazine, the 16th in the evening, the attacked baftion, and near half the adjoining curtain, was blown up, and above 800 men of the befieged. This misfortune obliged the commandant to capitulate the 19th at night. The garrifon, confifting of above 17,000 men, including 13 generals, and the fick and wounded at the two laft battles, were made prifoners of war.

GENERAL Driefen had been fent the 16th, with a body of troops, to befiege Lignitz; and, on the 26th, took that place by capitulation. Colonel Bulow, the governor, obtained leave to retire into Bohemia, with his garrifon, confifting of near 3000 men.

THUS one victory, improved by a vigorous and active genius, enabled his majefty to recover, in one month, all, excepting Schweidnitz, that he had loft during the whole campaign.

IT has been already obferved, that, when the king left Saxony, in order to go to Silefia, M. Keith, with about 8000 men, had been fent into Bohemia, with a view to draw general Marshal, then in Lufatia, there; and, by that means, facilitate the march of the king. This end having been happily accomplifhed, M. Keith, after he had burnt feveral magazines, and the bridge at Leutmeritz, returned into Saxony; where he put his troops into winter quarters.

REFLECTIONS

REFLECTIONS on the battle of Lissa, and the preceding operations.

PRINCE Charles knew, even before the battle of Breslaw, that the king, with about 10 or 12,000 men, at most, was coming into Silesia: the only object his majesty could have in view, was to join Bevern's army, without which he could attempt nothing at all; nor even, with so inconsiderable a force as that he brought with him, approach the Austrian army, without exposing himself to certain destruction. Wherefore, the only object prince Charles should have had in view, was to prevent him from effectuating this junction. His royal highness should therefore have marched to Parchwitz, and take a position between that place and Lignitz, with a strong corps, on the heights of Pfaffendorff, which would have hindered the king from approaching the Oder; nor even could he have gone to Glogau, without giving them an opportunity to attack him, and consequently defeat him, considering the Austrian army was, perhaps, six times stronger than he was.

THE only measure taken by the Austrians, was to send a garrison to Lignitz, which could answer no end whatever, and exposed so many men to be lost. It was by no means probable that the king would amuse himself with a siege of that miserable place, when all Silesia was at stake.

WHEN the Austrians had permitted the king to unite all his forces, and provide them with the necessary artillery, &c. we cannot conceive why all of a sudden they resolved to quit Breslaw, and go to meet him. I know very well, that flattery, too prevalent in camps, as well as courts, had raised their spirits and confidence much above what prudence prescribes: but they could then have no motives to desire an action; because, if victorious, they could not, in that advanced season, pursue the enemy further than Glogau; and, if vanquished, it might prove fatal to them.

HAVING

HAVING paſſed the Schweidnitz the 4th, they were informed the enemy was advancing towards them; Why not inſtantly repaſs that river, and put it before them, rather than behind Though this river is but ſmall, yet its banks, for the moſt part, are very marſhy; inſomuch that an army cannot paſs it without the greateſt difficulty, and ſcarce at all if they meet with any oppoſition. If the Auſtrians had done this, and have ſent a ſtrong corps higher up on their left flank, with their light troops on the ſame ſide as the enemy, on the road that leads to Striegau, we do not think his majeſty would have attempted to paſs the river; and, if he did, the corps abovementioned would have been on his flank during the paſſage and the action; and, as they were much ſtronger than he was, having their army covered by the Schweidnitz, they could have poſted 20,000 men on their flank; which would have made it impoſſible for the enemy to paſs the river. He would, therefore, in all probability, have marched to Striegau, in order to bring the Auſtrians from their advantageous ſituation, by endeavouring to cut off their communication with Bohemia. In this caſe, the corps, poſted, as we ſuppoſe, on their left, would have been at Striegau before the enemy; and the whole army muſt have marched behind Schweidnitz, with the right at Hohen Gierſdorff, and the left towards Friberg; which would have ſecured the road by Landſhut to Bohemia, and their communication with that country. This poſition is very ſtrong, and we do not think they could have been beat in it; nor, in that advanced ſeaſon, by any manœuvre on their left, be forced out of it; nor could the king continue in the neighbourhood of Striegau, having no magazines within a hundred miles of him. He muſt, therefore, have given up the point, and retire to Glogau, in order to refreſh his troops, who were much in need of reſt. Theſe meaſures being neglected, or never thought of, they ſhould have advanced, and occupied all

T   the

the hills before them, particularly that by Lobetnitz, as well to take this advantage from the enemy, as to have room enough behind them to manœuvre upon; but, from the moment they heard of the king's approach, they seem stupified; they neither advance nor retire. It is impossible for a superior army to be outwinged, but by some fault; yet this happened. The king made great demonstrations against their right, by which they were deceived so long, that he, covered by the hills they had neglected to occupy, had time to bring his whole army on their left. The only remedy then, was to order their right and center to march against his left; and, as they were much superior, and this wing weakened, to reinforce the right. They would have inveloped it, and in all probability destroyed it; nor could the king pursue his advantages on the right, while his left was thus attacked, for fear of being inclosed between the enemy's right wing and the river, where there was not ground enough to act in. They should, at the same time, have formed a line or two behind the flank attacked, with intervals to let the troops repulsed pass, and then advance against the enemy, whom they would have found broke, and in confusion, and, therefore, easily have defeated him.

INSTEAD of which, they ordered the whole army to make a motion on the left, to sustain that wing; so that the columns met their companions retiring, and the enemy advancing in order of battle; which hindered them from being able to form at all; and thus the whole army was defeated, one battalion after another, as must necessarily happen. Troops marching in small and long columns can never open, and form themselves in a line, when near the enemy, and under his fire; and, therefore, such a manœuvre must never be attempted. They should have endeavoured to keep the enemy back 'till they had formed a line, and then advance, or wait his coming. This not being executed, the battle was lost, and nothing could prevent it.

IT

IT was likewife a capital fault to have put the auxiliary troops, who had never feen an enemy, on the flank. If they had thrown their light troops, and 8 or 10 battalions of Auftrians, fuftained by Nadafti's corps, and the whole left wing, into the wood, before the village of Sagfchutz, and ordered their right and center to advance, and attack the enemy's left, we think they would have gained the victory.

THE king's conduct was founded on the moft fublime principles of war. Though his army was much inferior to that of the enemy, yet, by dint of fuperior manœuvres, he brought more men into action, at the point attacked, than they; which muft be decifive when the troops are nearly equal in goodnefs. Wherefore, generals muft make it their ftudy, to eftablifh, in time of peace, fuch evolutions as facilitate the manœuvres of armies; and, in time of war, choofe fuch a field of battle, if poffible, as enables them to hide part of their motions, and fo bring more men into action than the enemy; and, if the ground, either by its nature, or by the vigilance of the enemy, does not permit them to cover their motions, then a greater facility of manœuvring will anfwer the fame end, and enable them to bring more men to the principal point attacked than the enemy. The only advantage of a fuperior army, in a day of action, confifts in this only, that the general can bring more men into action than the enemy; but, if they do not move with facility and quicknefs, and are not all brought to action at the fame time, that fuperiority of numbers will be of no ufe: on the contrary, will ferve only to increafe the confufion. From whence we will deduce a general rule: " That general, who, by the facility
" of his motions, or by artifice, can bring moft men into action,
" at the fame time, and at the fame point, muft, if the troops are
" equally good, neceffarily prevail; and, therefore, all evolutions,
" which do not tend to this object, muft be exploded."

HISTORY of the WAR, &c.

OPERATIONS of the War in Pruſſia, between the Pruſſians and Ruſſians.

THE king of Pruſſia, being informed of the Czarina's acceſſion to the treaty of Verſailles, ordered general Lewhald, with about 30,000 men, to march on the frontiers of Pruſſia, and oppoſe the march of the enemy. Accordingly, this general, having aſſembled his army in the month of June, advanced to Inſterburg, with a corps further on towards Memel, to obſerve their motions.

IN the mean time, the Ruſſian army, conſiſting of 31 regiments of foot, 14 of horſe, 5 of huſſars, and about 16,000 Tartars, Calmucks, and Coſacks, amounting in the whole to 62,000 foot, 19,000 horſe, and the abovementioned Tartars, &c. broke up in May, and advanced, in four columns, towards the frontiers of Pruſſia.

THREE of which paſſed through Poland, and the fourth through Samogitia, towards Memel. This laſt was commanded by general Fermor, and deſtined to beſiege that town. To facilitate which enterprize, admiral Lewis, an Engliſhman of reputation, in the Ruſſian ſervice, ſailed with a conſiderable fleet from Revel, with about 9000 men on board, in order to land, and attack Memel on the ſea ſide, while general Fermor did the ſame on the land ſide. Accordingly, they arrived before Memel at the end of June, and, on the 5th of the following month, they took that place by capitulation.

THIS conqueſt was of infinite conſequence to the Ruſſians; becauſe they could make a convenient place of arms of it, and, by means of their fleet, provide it with proviſions and ſtores ſufficient to ſupply the whole army, (who could not poſſibly be provided otherwiſe) and conſequently proſecute the operations of the campaign.

THIS.

This expedition being happily executed, the whole army, under the command of M. Apraxin, united in the month of August, on the river Rufs; and from thence advanced towards the Pregel. Upon which general Lewhald quitted the camp at Infterburg, and retired towards Wehlau; where he continued 'till the 30th of August, and then advanced to attack the Ruffians, who had paffed the Pregel, and were encamped at Grofs Jagerfdorff. This occafioned a great battle: of which the Pruffians give the following account.

" Lieutenant general Schorlemmer having reconnoitred the ene-
" my's pofition, it was refolved to attack them the 30th. We
" firft attacked their left wing. Prince Holftein's regiment, under
" his own command, Ruefch's, and the fecond battalion of Schor-
" lemmer, diftinguifhed themfelves very much. They took feve-
" ral batteries, and totally defeated the enemy's cavalry. We
" advanced, over a prodigious number of dead bodies, againft the
" center and right wing of the enemy's army, that was protected
" by various batteries and retrenchments. We took three of them
" in the wood, each from 10 or 12 cannons: in one of which the
" marfhal himfelf gave quarter to a Ruffian colonel; and in ano-
" ther we made general Lapuchin prifoner. We fhould probably
" have kept the field of battle, if, unfortunately, our fecond line
" had not fired on our firft; the great fmoak of the artillery, and
" of two villages which the enemy had put on fire, having hin-
" dered our people from feeing their companions; fo that our firft
" line was expofed to the fire of the enemy's infantry, fuftained
" by 150 pieces of cannon, and that of our own fecond line. We
" therefore quitted the field of battle, and retired in good order,
" without being followed. Our lofs, in all, amounts to about
" 2000 men. That of the enemy much above 9000. Among
" whom are generals Lieven, and Lapuchin." This account, as
generally

in GERMANY, 1757.

generally happens with the losers, is very little exact, and no ways worthy to be printed, but impartiality required it.

THAT of M. Apraxin, to the Czarina, is as follows:

"I HAD the honour to inform your majesty, that numberless and invincible obstacles hindered us from approaching the enemy on the right of the Pregel. Wherefore, I resolved to pass this river, and force them to come to an action; which was accordingly done on the 28th; and, as the enemy perceived, by this manœuvre, and our ulterior march, that we could cut off their communication with the countries from whence they drew their subsistence, they found it necessary to abandon their strong camp, and likewise pass on our side the Pregel on the 28th. The 30th your majesty's army, in consequence of the order given the preceding night, was ready to march; and the vanguard, and part of the army, were already in motion; when, at 4 o'clock in the morning, we perceived that the wood, before our front, was filled with the enemy's troops, whose motions had been covered by it. We were not as yet formed, when the enemy came out of the wood in the finest order, and began to fire upon us with their artillery, and soon after with small arms; which continued without intermission the whole action. They attacked our front with great fury; and it required uncommon firmness to resist their efforts. The first and chief attack was against our left wing. They advanced in columns, within gun shot, and then formed the line. When both armies were formed, with the front against each other, the fire of artillery and small arms continued for three hours, and the victory was all this while doubtful. The enemy made all the efforts possible to break our front, but were repulsed in each attempt with great loss. While these things passed on our left, they attacked our right and vanguard (who, from the

" nature of the ground, were somewhat more advanced than our
" left) with two separate corps of cavalry, sustained by infan-
" try; but were repulsed in both places. Our artillery, particu-
" larly those called the Schwalows, did great execution; and
" contributed much to throw the enemy's cavalry in confusion.
" Though they met every where with the same bad success, they
" made one effort more. On our left wing several openings were
" found in the line, because the marshy ground made it impracti-
" cable to close it. The enemy attempted to penetrate through
" these intervals, in order to cut our line in two, and so take it
" in flank; but they were mistaken: for we had posted there
" some troops out of the second line; so that, scarce had they
" entered the wood, when they were received with fixed bayon-
" nets, and soon forced to fly with precipitation: which put an
" end to the battle, &c."

The rest of general Apraxin's letter contains nothing more than compliments, no wise necessary to give an idea of the action.

The Russians took 29 cannons, and about 600 prisoners. Their loss consisted in 800 killed, among which were generals Lapuchin, Sybin, and Kapnist; and 4260 wounded, among whom were the generals Lieven, Tolstoi, Bosquet, Villeboy, Manteuffel, Weimarn, and Plemannikow. That of the Prussians in about 3000 killed, wounded, and missing.

The Prussians retired to Wehlau, and the Russians continued in their camp, by Norkitten, 'till the 7th of September; when they made some dispositions, as if they intended passing the river Aller, at Friedland, on the enemy's right flank; but it was not executed. They attempted likewise to disembark some troops in the Curish bay, but were repulsed by the militia. On the 17th the whole Russian army broke up, and retired in haste towards the frontiers; so that, by the end of the month, they had entirely

abandoned

abandoned the kingdom of Pruſſia, excepting Memel; where they left 10 or 12,000 men. This put an end to the campaign in Pruſſia.

REFLECTIONS.

WHEN the Pruſſians knew that the enemy was in march, they ſhould, one would think, advance to the frontiers, and have made incurſions into Poland, to deſtroy the proviſions, or carry it off; which would have retarded very much the progreſs of the enemy, who had abſolutely no other means of ſubſiſting, but what they found on the ſpot, as they paſſed; which was rendered ſtill more difficult, by the terror the Tartars inſpired, by their uncommon ravages and cruelty. Another advantage would have accrued; that the inhabitants of Pruſſia would have had time to withdraw themſelves, and their cattle, and retire to Konigſberg, or ſome other places of ſurety: whereas, by ſtaying on the Pregel, the beſt part of the country was left at the mercy of the enemy.

As to the conduct of the action itſelf, nothing can be objected to M. Lewhald. He had, no doubt, orders to fight, though much inferior. He formed his army in a line, facing the enemy, which may be conſidered as a fault, being ſo much weaker than they; becauſe he could not make any conſiderable effort, in any one point; his troops being equally diſtributed throughout the line; ſo that the enemy had every where a greater number of men in action than he could have. As the Ruſſians were then little known, 'tis no wonder the Pruſſian general ſhould think his troops ſuperior to theirs, and therefore did not think it neceſſary to oppoſe any thing but infantry to infantry, and cavalry againſt cavalry. But experience has proved, that the Ruſſian infantry is by far ſuperior to any in Europe; inſomuch that I queſtion whether it can be defeated by any other infantry whatever; and, as their cavalry is not so good as that of other nations, reason dictates, that a mixed order of battle alone can conquer them. They cannot be defeated; they must be killed; and infantry, mixed with great corps of cavalry, only can do this.

If the Russians intended to remain in Prussia, their first care ought to have been to form magazines at Memel, in order to supply the army; because they must know, that it was impossible for the country, even had they observed the most exact discipline, to furnish enough for that purpose. The want of this precaution, both this and all the following campaigns, rendered their victories useless. They made war, and always will, in all probability, like the Tartars. They will over-run a country, ravage and destroy it, and so leave it; because they can never, according to the method they now follow, make a solid and lasting conquest. They put themselves an insurmountable barrier to it. Their own light troops, and the want of a solid plan of operations, will one day ruin their army.

OPERATIONS of the War in Pomerania, between the Pruſſians and Swedes.

THE Swedes, under pretence of guarrantying the treaty of Weſtphalia, ſent an army of about 17,000 men, under the command of general Ungern Stornberg, againſt the Pruſſians. This army paſſed the Peen, and, having ſoon taken Demmin, Anclam, and the iſlands of Uſedom and Wollin, they advanced into the Pruſſian part of Pomerania; where they raiſed contributions, without meeting any obſtacle: for the garriſon of Stettin, conſiſting of about 10,000 men, under general Manteuffel, could not quit that important place, in order to oppoſe the progreſs of the Swedes. At length, however, the army, which had been in Pruſſia, arrived under general Lewhald; and, before the end of December, forced the Swedes to abandon all they had taken, except the Penamunder and the Anclamer retrenchments, and retire under the cannon of Stralſund.

Thus ended the campaign of 1757, the moſt important for the number of great actions, the variety of events, and the uncertainty of its iſſue, of any recorded either in antient or modern hiſtory.

We hope our account of it, and our reflections on its various operations, will prove no leſs agreeable than uſeful to our readers.

The End of the First Volume.

www.ingramcontent.com/pod-product-compliance
Lightning Source LLC
Chambersburg PA
CBHW020847160426

43192CB00007B/820